21 DOORS
A TAROT STORY

21 DOORS
A TAROT STORY

Where real life flows
through the wisdom
of the Tarot

JO GALLOWAY

PILLARS OF DIVINITY
Birdwood, New South Wales

21 DOORS, A TAROT STORY

Paperback ISBN: 978-0-646-86752-6

Published by Pillars of Divinity
Birdwood, New South Wales
Printed in Australia
First Edition, December 2022

Cover Design by: VeryMuchSo Agency
Interior Layout by: Make Your Mark Publishing Solutions
Editing by: Lyric Dodson

Acknowledgements

This book would not be possible without the confidence of my good friend, Kristine Gibson. The word gratitude does not begin to express my feelings. A special universal thank you for your encouragement, wisdom, and insightful criticism. Your tireless support was invaluable in making a better book.

Thank you also to Lyric Dodson for bringing this story together and to my publishing manager, Monique Mensah, (Make Your Mark Publishing Solutions), for supporting me to produce *21 Doors, A Tarot Story* to be the best book it could be.

Thank you to my amazing husband, Ken, for your love, support, and lost hours together while I wrote this book. Thank you for believing in me and my work. I love you, and I am blessed to have you in my life. Husbands don't come any better than you.

Finally, thank you to all my teachers throughout my tarot journey.

Dedicated to my father, my King of Wands.
You are always in my heart.

Introduction

This is a Tarot book unlike any other you may have read or studied, a book you'll be glad you had at the start of your Tarot journey. Other Tarot books teach history, symbolism, card meanings, and spreads in matter-of-fact terms. All of these topics are great and a definite need-to-know, but *21 Doors, A Tarot Story* will teach you the meanings held within each of the seventy-eight Tarot cards using everyday scenarios. This will allow you to recall the meanings more quickly so your intuition can flow freely and help you deliver accurate, reliable readings.

The mythology behind *21 Doors, A Tarot Story* is that there is no inherent meaning in an individual event. The only meaning is the importance we give to it. For example, let's say you have planned a lovely garden wedding. On the morning of your big day, you wake up to find it is raining. In this case, the rain is the event. The meaning you may give to this event is one of disappointment, sadness, and anger. Now, picture you are a farmer living through a three-year drought. You wake up one morning to find it is raining. Now, the meaning you attach to this event (rain) is one of delight, happiness, and joy. It's the same event with a different meaning.

The same principle applies to Tarot cards. Some cards may depict similar energies but have different meanings according to different readers. There is no one way to read the cards; therefore, you can never get it wrong. Coming up with your own meanings instead of trying to remember other people's interpretations is of upmost importance. In addition, illustrating your own personal Tarot card interpretation by way of a real-life event can help foster greater cognitive memory association. In other words, the card interpretation will be absorbed into your subconscious mind, and it will be easier for you to recall it later during a reading. This effectively allows your intuition to flow freely and at a higher vibration.

As an experienced hypnotherapist, I've joined together my psychology knowledge with my thirty years of Tarot study to create a method that can make memorising the card meanings simple and easy. I have achieved this by attaching a Tarot meaning to a real-life event. Our mind will first remember the event, then bring to conscious awareness the meaning we attached to said event. For example, whenever I am presented with the Fool (which traditionally symbolises one stepping into the unknown) in a reading, my subconscious mind will recall a time I left my secure job to move across country to start an exciting, new chapter (the event). All the emotions, thoughts, and aspirations related to this event is what I remember most. Therefore, I'm able to connect that time in my life to the symbolism of that card for quicker recall.

Within *21 Doors, A Tarot Story*, you will learn the meanings of each card by following Tom and Karen's enlightening travels through the Minor Arcana—Wands, Pentacles, Cups, and Swords—and each of the twenty-one doors of the Major Arcana. This book will take you through some of the day-to-day events most people experience throughout life, from falling in love to starting a business to buying a home and raising children. This book was written as a guide to walk you through each suit and arcana and help you make associations to the cards that will stick in your subconscious mind. This is not a tutorial on how to read Tarot cards, nor will you find any spreads to follow. There are many books that can help you learn these topics, but the purpose of this book is to help you memorise the meanings of the cards with ease.

As you journey with Tom and Karen, you will recognize similarities as the patterns resonate with your own life's path, therefore enhancing your connection with the cards. As you follow along, keep a journal handy so you can write down one or two keywords or phrases that resonate with you for each card. I have added a short list of keywords, phrases, and further interpretations after each card. If you're looking for another resource to help you learn how to read spreads, you can grab a copy of my free e-book *Beginner's Guide to Reading Tarot Cards*, which includes six printable keyword charts. You can find all of this information on my website: pillarsofdivinity.com.

Not only do we learn by connecting a meaning to an event, but we also learn through visualisation. Therefore, along with each segment of the story, I have included a visual representation of the corresponding card from the popular Rider Waite Tarot deck to help you make associations with the symbolism. As you follow Tom and Karen's life adventures, you may begin to physically feel the meanings. This is yet another tool that can help you implant the card's meaning into your subconscious mind.

By the end of this book, you will have a working knowledge of the cards and perhaps even a few associations you've made yourself along the way. In time, you will be able to interpret every card without having to reference guidebooks, so you can give an accurate reading with confidence every time.

Before we begin, let's get familiar with your Tarot deck so you know exactly what you're working with. In a traditional Tarot deck, there are seventy-eight cards divided into two parts. Twenty-two cards make up the Major Arcana (Majors), which represents big, important life events from birth until death. These cards symbolise the physical, spiritual, intellectual, and emotional aspects of life and the universe. The remaining fifty-eight cards that make up the Minor Arcana represent the day-to-day, mundane events we may deal with and can potentially tell us the best way to handle them. The Major Arcana represents the overarching energy, perspective, or guidance needed to navigate the "smaller" events of the Minor Arcana.

Like a deck of regular playing cards, the Minor Arcana is broken into four suits, with each containing four court cards and ten numbered cards. Each suit touches on a general aspect of our daily lives.

The Wands are represented by the element of fire and correspond to the clubs in a regular playing card deck. The Wands symbolise all the things that keep you busy during the course of a day, be it work, home life, or the great outdoors. Wands represent ideas, growth, ambition, and expansion. They show

how our original thoughts are seeds through which life springs. In other words, they talk about our actions, creativity, and passions. The Wands also correlate to the fire zodiac signs Aries, Leo, and Sagittarius.

The Pentacles correlate to the element of earth and the diamonds in a regular playing card deck. The Pentacles represent the external, physical level of consciousness, including material possessions, industry, business, commerce, trade, finances, property, home, nature, and security. It also represents manifestation, realisation, hard facts, and general prosperity, mirroring the outer situations of your health, finances, and work in every sense. The Pentacles are closely related to the earth zodiac signs Taurus, Virgo, and Capricorn.

Following the Pentacles, we have the Cups. The Cups in the Tarot are likened to the hearts in a regular playing card deck and represent the element of water. They deal with the emotional level of consciousness, including love, moods, and dreams. The Cups mirror our spontaneous responses and habitual reactions to situations. Since water is a symbol of the subconscious mind and reason, the Cups are associated with anything emotional, from relationships (both professional and personal) to personal keepsakes and concerns. This suit corresponds with the water zodiac signs Pisces, Cancer, and Scorpio.

Last is the suit of Swords, which corresponds to the spades in a regular playing card deck and is represented by the alchemistic, ethereal air element. This suit deals heavily with the mental level of consciousness, including thoughts, intellect, quality of mind, attitudes, and beliefs. The Swords represent the mind, rationality, and power, which is found in its two-edged appearance. As such, intellect and power can be used for either good or ill and must be balanced by spirit and feeling. The Swords correspond symbolically to the air zodiac signs Aquarius, Libra, and Gemini.

To summarise, the Wands represent creativity, action, and passion (what we do). The Pentacles represent possessions and the material world (what we have). The Cups are associated with emotions, feelings, and relationships (what we feel). And the Swords represent our mental state, intellect, and thoughts (what we think).

In each suit, there are four court cards. There is a lot of confusion surrounding these cards in the Tarot community. Some say they are personality cards, and while I agree, as they each hold true to the essence of the suit in which they belong, I also see them as a progression in maturity. The Page represents a child, youth, or the early stages of a project. The Knight is a messenger, an immature adult, or a teenager who is full of vigour and ready to take action. The Queen is more mature in their views on life and possesses nurturing qualities, while the King is wise, powerful, and a leader. They know what they want and how to obtain it. Bear in mind, a Queen is not necessarily feminine, nor is a King masculine; all of the court cards can represent someone who is female, male, neither, or both.

It could be a little easier to remember the role of the court cards if you think of them hierarchically. The Page is a seeker who is young at heart and is often formulating the early stages of a creative, wild venture. The Knight acts on the Page's idea. Here, the project or opportunity begins to gain some momentum. The Queen accepts the offer presented by the Knight but uses their emotional maturity to decide what feels intuitively right. The King is the highest on the totem pole. Their feelings and ideas are real, valid, and can be trusted. There is no fluff with the King. The creativity born in the Page grew with the Knight and was deciphered with the Queen so the King could take solid, certain actions. Everyone works together.

Now that you have a general idea of the four suits and the court cards, let's talk about each numbered card. When I first began reading the Tarot, I found it incredibly helpful to associate each number with a particular general meaning. This is called numerology, the study of numbers that has been used in many cultures for thousands of years. It's important to note as well that these numbered cards, like the rest of the Tarot, tell a story and build on one another. It's been said the Tarot is a story in motion.

According to what I've learned over the years, aces represent new beginnings, potential, and inspiration. Twos symbolise the collaboration of the ideas started with the ace; they are focused on decisions and finding balance. Threes represent the essence of the ace's idea and the two's balance coming together for growth and completion, like when a couple births a child. Fours symbolise stability and a set foundation for our goals. With the fives, we meet chaos, conflict, and change. Sometimes it's welcomed change, and other times, it's less than desirable. In the sixes, we find harmony, healing, and alignment, and we begin to move away from the conflicts we experienced with five. Sevens indicate a time of pause and reflection, a time to assess and re-evaluate our plans. Eights represent growth and movement, a time to master, reap, and sow. Nines represent attainment and wish fulfilment, for we are almost done with this chapter of life, and the tens symbolise the finale, the end of a cycle.

Again, I encourage you to create a Tarot journal so you can take notes of any interpretations, keywords, or phrases you think of as you read along. This will help further cement the cards' meanings in your subconscious mind, thus creating your own personal memory bank. I hope you enjoy this journey.

I

THE WANDS

THE WANDS

"From a little spark bursts a flame."
—Dante Alighieri

We begin *A Tarot Story* at the beginning of Tom and Karen's life adventures with the suit of Wands. The Wands represent the fire element and have qualities of energetic enthusiasm, creativity, and inspiration. These cards exude optimism, excitement, and confidence. Their spiritual lesson is for you to maintain passion and energy toward your goals.

Ace of Wands

The sun was *beginning* to descend below the horizon as a soft breeze cooled the air. It wasn't cold enough for a jacket, but there was a slight chill, nonetheless. The first sign of spring had finally arrived, following a cold, bleak winter. On his way home from work, Tom noticed that the trees alongside the street were beginning to bud with *new growth*. The bees were busy doing their thing, and the air had a *new, fresh feel*. Spring was Tom's favourite season. He loved to witness the emergence of *new life* around and within him.

Once he arrived home, Tom grabbed a cold beer from the fridge and slumped down on the still-warm concrete steps on his back porch. He'd had another hard, stressful day working as a mechanic at the local garage, where he had been employed for ten long years. Tom could hear his beautiful wife Karen making dinner in the kitchen through the open window above him. He had a good life and was still madly in love with his wife. His feelings for her had not diminished one bit since the day they met all those years ago. Her long, flowing, blonde hair and her deep turquoise eyes summoned him on the wet, chilly afternoon when they first met. Never had he seen a girl so pretty. He knew right then and there that she was the one for him.

These nostalgic thoughts made Tom realise that he had a lot for which to be grateful. The couple almost owned their home outright, and Tom had been fortunate enough to be able to save a little for a rainy day. But for quite a while, Tom had been feeling despondent to all the good in his life. He *yearned for something more*. At the end of each long, tiresome day, Tom arrived home feeling flat, defeated, and uninspired. Karen was beginning to worry about him. She noticed that he had dropped a fair amount of weight recently, probably because he hardly finished his meals. He looked pale, drawn, and the black circles under his eyes were becoming quite obvious. Even Karen's mother, Dot, made a comment to her about him recently. Tom had even begun to neglect his personal appearance and would go days without shaving. This was a real red flag for Karen because Tom had always valued his health and appearance. The once neat and tidy man now looked unkempt and bedraggled. He did not look well at all, and Karen knew something was wrong, but she said nothing. She knew Tom would tell her what was troubling him when he thought the time was right.

Enjoying his cold beer, Tom reflected back to his child-hood, mainly to his grandmother, Nana Flo (or Gran, as she was more fondly called). Tom thought about his grandmother's glorious mane of silver hair. When she let it out of its usual tight bun, it flowed halfway down her back. As a small boy, Tom loved sitting by the fire watching Gran brush her hair before she went to bed at night. Gran had many sayings that would often get Tom thinking, as she was a very wise old lady. He loved and missed her immensely and often thought of those childhood summers he spent with her and pops on their farm.

Gran had a saying: "Once a thought, take a chance. Twice a thought, you better listen. But three times a thought, you better act or you'll be a-missing." Tom sighed at his youthful ignorance and regretted not listening to his "silent guidance system," which Gran said was within us all. The thought of leaving his job and *branching out on his own* had crossed his mind more than a dozen times over the past few months. Gran would be disappointed that he did not act sooner, but he was sure she would understand his reservations; he simply had not been feeling like his usual, positive, enthusiastic self lately. Work had really started to pull him down. Even the love Tom had for his wife and children could not pull him out from under the black clouds he felt were looming too close for comfort. Tom felt like there had to be more to life. He knew deep within he was meant for something greater; he just didn't know what to do. But he was also wise, and he knew that the time had come for him to *take action*. "Deeds not words" was another one of Gran's favourite sayings.

Tom was a good mechanic, but he had lost his spark for the job he once found so fulfilling. He had always put his family first and worried that his *new ideas* of branching out on his own would put them at risk. He was a good husband

and a wonderful provider. Everyone who knew Tom and Karen respected and admired them.

Tom loved his family above all else and devoted his weekends to spending quality time with them. He never missed his eight-year-old son Isac's Saturday soccer games. He even volunteered to step in and help coach if the trainer was away or sick. He absolutely adored his gentle, supporting wife and treasured his children but still felt like something was missing. He struggled to put his thoughts into words and explain to Karen what he was feeling. He knew she was worried and that the time had come for him to open up to her.

Lately, Tom had been thinking deeply about *starting his own business*, an idea that had always appealed to him. He wanted to be his own boss and call the shots. He was tired of working to fill someone else's pockets. Tom knew the way to help himself and his family was to work for himself. That way, he could have greater control over their future. Tom also liked the idea of connecting more with people. Spending his workdays under a car had become very lonely. He was willing to take the risk and reap the rewards. Tom felt like *the timing was right*.

While sitting outside, enjoying some quiet time, Tom thought about how he should approach the subject with Karen. He could almost feel his gran gently nudging him in his back to get on with it. Finishing the last of his beer, he casually walked back inside to the kitchen and wrapped his arms around the woman who had supported him through most of his adult life. Karen turned around and smiled. It quickly faded as the feeling sunk in that something still was not quite right.

"Tom, what's the matter?" she whispered, as not to alarm

their four-year-old daughter, Alice, who sat at the dinner table dreamily doodling in her colouring book.

"I have been thinking a lot lately about leaving my job and branching out to start my own business," he said.

Karen knew her husband well and hugged him tighter, knowing he had thought this over long and hard before saying anything. She was silently relieved that he had finally opened up to her.

"Let's finish dinner, and after the kids have gone to bed, tell me what you are thinking," she said.

With the dishes washed and put away and the kids tucked in for the night, Karen made Tom and herself a hot cup of coffee. They sat down at the kitchen table together, and Karen held Tom by the hand to reassure him that she was listening and he had her full support. She could feel the *enthusiasm* in Tom's demeanour and couldn't help but feel excited for him. She sensed that he was struggling to find the right words, but she did not rush him.

"Well," Tom started, feeling a little anxious about Karen's reaction. "You know that old, run-down store at the end of the street, the one with the broken window?" Karen nodded. "Well, I have been thinking of opening up a spare parts store. At work, we have most of our spare parts shipped in, and there is a huge profit to be made on each part. Labour is usually only half the cost of the repairs. I could supply all the garages in our area and maybe even sell online." Tom was brimming with excitement as he told Karen his plans.

Karen did not say a word; instead, she let Tom explain all his ideas. When he finished, she tightly squeezed his hand and told him to go for it. She thought it was a wonderful idea, and she trusted his judgment; Tom was generally not one to make foolish decisions. Karen loved to see him full of creative energy and passion for life once again. Tom picked her up and swung her around the kitchen.

"I've never seen you so happy, not since the day Isac was born," Karen said, laughing. She was so happy to have her old Tom back at last.

Tom put her down and said, "Do you have any pie? I think I would like some now." Karen smiled and got out two plates and a tub of ice cream from the freezer. They sat in silence, both lost in their own thoughts.

The next morning, Tom woke up raring to go. He kissed Karen before he got out of bed and whispered, "I am leaving early so I have time to get a closer look at the store before I start work."

With every idle moment at work that day, his thoughts drifted to how good his business could be. Tom began to launch himself wholeheartedly into his *new endeavour*, brimming with *confidence, drive, ambition,* and *enthusiasm.* The time was right to *put his plans into action*, and he had a strong feeling that *anything was possible*. He was *motivated to begin making huge changes in his life*, and he felt Gran right behind him, urging him on.

"You don't need to know the whole plan," Gran would say. "One foot knows how to follow the other if you have faith."

Keywords/Phrases: Beginnings, new path, new life, yearn for something more, branch out, take action, new ideas, starting own business, timing is right, enthusiasm, creative energy, raring to go, confidence, drive, ambition, plans into action, anything is possible.

Further Interpretations: Dream big, strong physical energy, a spark of inspiration, opportunity knocks, enthusiastic creative force, inspired action.

Visual Reprensentation: When you first look at the Ace of Wands, you'll notice the hand of opportunity offering you a wand. Aces represent new beginnings, and this wand is budding with new life and growth, causing Tom to feel inspired and excited about his new business idea. The Ace of Wands is the beginning, a fresh start, the spark of creative energy needed to branch out on a new and exciting adventure. This is the upsurge of new energies that tells you anything is possible. Tom acknowledges that the spark of inspiration offered by the Ace is a sign that he is co-creating with spirit, and it would be wise to listen. Gran often reminded him as a young boy to allow his higher self to guide him. "Your higher self knows your destiny and will continue to steer you where you need to go," she'd say.

Two of Wands

Tom's mind was in a spin from all the things he had to think about. The constant whirlwind of thoughts and ideas were causing him to make mistakes at work and lose his concentration. One afternoon at work, one of the young apprentices working at the garage stopped Tom just in time before he added the wrong fluid to a car's engine. Tom had also begun misdiagnosing car problems, which made for a lot of unhappy clients. His boss, Tony, had even expressed some concern, asking him if he felt OK. He simply wasn't acting like himself. For the next few nights, Tom tossed and turned until the sun came up, getting no more than one hour of sleep each night.

"Am I doing the right thing?" he asked Karen one morning with tired eyes.

She quickly assured him that if it felt right, he was on the right track.

"You know your gran would tell you the same. We don't get these urges of inspiration for no reason. The universe is trying to tell you something. I think it would be wise to listen," she said.

Tom was beginning to realize that his *dreams could actually become a reality*. He still had many *decisions to make*, but he *had faith* he would make the right ones when the time came.

"I have *so much to think about and do before I can actually put my plans into action* and open the doors of my shop," he told Karen.

"Lean on me if you need a hand; I would love to help," she replied.

Tom *couldn't predict if his store would be a success or a failure, but he believed in his vision enough to give it a try.* With Karen's support, he felt like *anything was possible.* Gran always said, "*Be clear* on what you want because if you can hold it in your mind and hold it in your heart, you will hold it in your hand."

Over the course of following week, Tom began to pull himself together and settle his thoughts. He needed to plan out his next moves. Over breakfast, Tom asked Karen if she could purchase a planner so he could begin to *formulate a solid plan* on how best to move forward. The first thing he decided to do was make a few phone calls during his lunch break at work. First, he called the real estate agency to inquire about whether or not the storefront he had his eye on was available for lease and what the monthly rent was. This was the first hurdle he had to face because if the price of the storefront was not within his budget, he would have to look elsewhere. Although he recognized he had a lot of *tough choices to make*, he was not going to let anything stand between him and his ambitions. He would open his store by any means necessary.

Tom was beginning to put his *plans into action*, and all his ideas were *coming together.* Next on Tom's to-do list was to contact the company his boss bought parts from to see if they would be interested in supplying his store, then he wanted to call other garages in his area to ask if they would do business with him if he was to open a local store. In the midst of all this, Karen recognized that, despite having a lot on his plate, Tom was in *high spirits* again, and for that, she was grateful.

To Tom and Karen's surprise, the business idea received tons of support and generated more interest than either of them imagined. It was beginning to look as if his business idea had quite a bit of *potential*. Tom knew his success depended on his *courage, drive, and determination* to take on this challenge and *put his faith in his abilities* to see it through. All the while, Karen was right behind him, encouraging him to *follow his heart*. With her love and support, Tom was able to *conjure up the energy and vitality* he needed to accomplish his dreams.

A few days after his initial call, the real estate agency returned Tom's call with good news. Not only was the store available, but it was listed at a price well below Tom's expectations. By this time, the bank had approved Tom's application for a loan to buy stock for the store, and most of the suppliers he'd contacted were more than happy to set up an account and supply him with parts. *His plan was slowly coming together*, and he was excited to see where it would go. Karen was excited too because they had decided she would work in the office and handle all the books. Together, they made a *great team*.

Karen knew this new journey would inspire them both; she had always wanted them to work side by side. Although she loved every second of rearing their two beautiful children, her days at home with them were long. She knew the time was right, as Alice was growing fast, Isac was already in school, and her hours working in the shop would be flexible enough for her to be home every day when Isac got home. She was her own boss and could come and go as she pleased, but she was *prepared to put in the necessary hours* to help Tom make his business a success.

One night, after dinner was cleaned up and the children were in bed, Tom asked Karen once again if he was doing the right thing. She looked up from the book she was reading, surprised at his question. He had been so *full of faith and enthusiasm*, but she figured that since his *dream was quickly becoming a reality*, he could be having cold feet. Karen was pleased to see Tom step up after his depressive episode had passed. His new business idea gave him his confidence back so he could once again stand tall and be proud of the man he was.

"What do you think?" Karen asked in reply. "What do you feel? What would Nana Flo say?"

Tom sat quietly for a few moments, then said, "Nana Flo would say to go for it." That was all the encouragement he needed. He got up and gave Karen the biggest hug before heading off to bed with renewed confidence.

That night, Tom had the best sleep he'd had in months. Ever since he first told Karen about his thoughts, he felt an immense amount of confidence, and he was now positive that he had made the right decision. He was thoroughly comforted by the thought of his Gran pulling strings for him in the afterlife, helping everything to fall into place.

"Be clear on what you want," Gran would say. "And ask for help. Not from the living, but from your angels." Gran was a great believer in spirit guides and always trusted that angels

had her back. "Never lose faith; allow the universe to do for you what you cannot do for yourself. Always ask for guidance when you feel stuck." Fond memories of Gran came flooding back to Tom as he laid in bed, rested and happy. The decision was made. Before he drifted off to sleep, he mumbled to himself, "Go for it."

Keywords/Phrases: Ideas coming together, progress, partnership, plans into action, decision, choices to make, duality, faith, hope.

Further Interpretations: A time for compromise, travel plans, fresh ideas, power position, plan next move, trust your dreams and the process.

Visual Representation: Looking at the Two of Wands card, you'll notice that one of the Wands is firmly planted on the ground. This represents Tom putting his inspired ideas from the Ace into action. The other wand is still in the air, which could signify that Tom still has decisions to make. He holds the world in his hand, his ideas hold promise, and anything is possible. The Two of Wands shows the early stages of Tom's plans. There are a lot of choices to make. Together, Tom and Karen form a great partnership and make some progress. This is a time for Tom to be clear and focused and draw on his inner strength and faith. Tom is aware that he is being divinely guided.

Three of Wands

In this moment, Tom's *plans were beginning to look promising*, and all of his research and hard work were *beginning to pay off.* Tom knew the time was right to resign from his job, much to Tony's surprise. He hung on for as long as he could, but he could no longer afford to spend eight hours of his day at work and away from his new venture. If his business was going to be a success, he had to jump in feet first. It was all or nothing. He had a little money saved, and with his new bank loan and Karen's *support*, he knew he would be OK.

To Tom's surprise, Tony was highly supportive and stood behind him 100 percent. He offered Tom some part-time work until things at the store got off the ground, which Tom graciously accepted. He decided to take the plunge and use his and Karen's savings to lease the old, abandoned building. He and Karen spent the next week feverishly painting and repairing the store back to its former glory. Then, he began ordering stock and filling shelves that he purchased at a local discount store. His *enthusiasm was at an all-time high*, and all the right contacts were appearing to him *as if by magic.* Tom knew his Gran was watching out for him.

The morning of the grand opening, Tom and Karen awoke early. Their nervous tension was palpable; neither of them said much over breakfast. They showered and dressed in the new embroidered work shirts Karen had ordered specifically for this special day. Tom's shirt was navy blue, while Karen's was a soft pink. They both looked the part. After dropping Isac at school and Alice at day care, they arrived at the store a half hour before it was set to open. Tom told Karen he was feeling extremely anxious.

"What if no one shows up?" he asked. Karen gave him a warm-hearted hug and reassured him that everything was going to be fine, even though she was feeling the same way. Right at 8:30 a.m., Tom and Karen opened the doors to their new store, and the business was officially *up and running*. Tom stepped into his new position of store proprietor with confidence. Their first customers arrived, and everything ran smoothly. Karen was amazed at just how confidently Tom handled his first sales. He even managed to work the new till like a pro. Even though the store was now open, there was still a lot of hard work to do, but Tom remained *optimistic*, especially since the business was *showing promising signs*.

During a break in customers and ringing phones, Tom and Karen's eyes met, and they exchanged smiles. Karen found it hard to hold back her tears of joy in that moment. She knew this was only *the beginning of a long journey*, but she was excited to *watch their ships come in* as their business grew. They were both aware that patience was needed and there was no reason to panic. The best was yet to come.

Karen was delighted to take on the job of bookkeeper in addition to looking after the children. She was a real natural with numbers and was just as *inspired and dedicated* to the business as Tom was. She loved being involved, even if only part-time. Not to mention, the job gave her the opportunity to spend more time with Tom. Karen now felt like she had a *purpose* and some *direction* with her free time. Tom had always said Karen was the one with *vision and foresight* between the two of them. Together, they made an unstoppable force.

In the days following the grand opening, many of the couple's friends sent cards and flowers. A few turned up at closing time to have a drink and toast to their success. Tony even dropped in one night to wish Tom and Karen his best and offer Tom some sound advice. In bed that night, Tom told Karen just how much everyone's support meant to him. Karen was also blown away by the love she felt from people she didn't even know around town. She told Tom about a few of the mothers at Isac's school who congratulated her and wished her all the best. The amount of support they felt from their community made the couple that much more motivated to see their store become a success. Just before they drifted off to sleep, Tom held Karen tight and whispered, "We make a great team."

The business was still in its *early days*, open for just over a month, and Tom was beginning to feel confident that all his hard work was worth it and his business would be a success. He was grateful for the support of his family and friends, but secretly worried if he could continue on such a high and stand the test of time. Tom laid awake some nights wondering if he and his business would survive all the trials and tribulations that he knew were sure to follow. He knew that only time would tell.

Tom knew the time was quickly approaching when he would need to travel to *expand his horizons*. He needed to secure more suppliers and begin researching for better stock-purchasing options. Tom accepted the fact that it would take some time for him to see a return on his and Karen's initial investment. They had used all their savings to get the store up and running. Luckily, their first month of business was an *astounding success*. It seemed as though *everything was going to plan*, and *the right contacts were appearing out of the blue* to support the growth of their business. Things were looking good, and Karen and Tom had every reason to remain optimistic.

Now, at the end of the day, Tom was able to sit outside on his favourite step and smile, feeling happy with where his life was heading. Those past feelings of despair had completely disappeared.

"I feel like I am finally *fulfilling my soul's purpose* and living *in alignment* with my path," he told Karen that night in bed. "Gran would be so proud of us."

Karen smiled, wrapped her arm around her wonderful husband, snuggled in close, and drifted off to sleep.

Keywords/Phrases: Plans are promising, hard work pays off, support from others, enthusiasm, right contacts, up and running, optimistic, only the beginning, waiting for your ship to come in, inspired, purpose, direction, dedicated, vision and foresight, early days, expansion, success, fulfilling.

Further Interpretations: Travel to learn new things, step into the unknown with confidence, teamwork, expand your vision, new opportunities on the horizon, planning your next move.

Visual Representation: Tom and Karen have acted on their creative energy and are moving forward. The Three of Wands signifies that they are at the end of the first phase of their journey but still have lots more to look forward to. They realise they are the creators of their own world. Although it is only the early days, they are optimistic that they will be successful. Now, they must keep working and wait for their ships to come in. Tom has set the wheels in motion, and now it is time to let the universe do the rest. At this stage of the journey, Tom and Karen are looking ahead to the future. From here, they can step into the unknown with confidence and begin to think even bigger.

Four of Wands

The store had been open for about a year now, and the books were finally beginning to show a small profit. Many of the local and regional garages were now coming to Tom's store for their parts. Their range of stock had grown considerably since the couple first opened their doors. Every day a new supplier rep popped in to offer their products. It got to the point where Tom had to become a little more selective with what he bought for the store, as he only wanted to supply the very best for his customers.

The town rallied behind them to show its support. It was clear to everyone that Tom and Karen made a *great team*. The store was running smoothly, which gave Tom very little to worry about. In fact, the couple's work environment was incredibly even-keeled, with neither of them feeling like the boss and both understanding that for the store to be a success and operate effectively, each of them had to make sacrifices. Karen forewent her weekly tennis matches so she could devote her time to bookkeeping. Life for her would definitely be more relaxed once Alice started school next fall. As hard as it was, Tom explained to Isac why he could no longer be there for his Saturday morning soccer games. Isac was disappointed but understood. Karen knew this broke both of their hearts.

The store had been good to them during that first year, and Tom felt it was time for a little *celebration*. With the store experiencing some newfound stability, it was the perfect time for the family to relax a little, considering they hadn't taken a single day off since opening. First, Tom decided to make reservations for a Friday night date with Karen. They had a wonderful night dining at a beautiful Italian restaurant, celebrating the first of many years of success. Before their meal arrived, they made a toast to their store and financial security as well as *gave thanks and gratitude* for all they had achieved so far.

Tom also booked a weekend getaway for the entire family. The couple spent a wonderful weekend lazing by the pool at the Flash Hotel resort, while the kids had a blast splashing in the water. Nine-year-old Isac spent a good part of the weekend teaching five-year-old Alice how to swim. Karen and Tom were amazed at how patient and gentle he was with her and took a moment to talk about how proud they were of their children.

Tom had always said that Isac was a clone of Nana Flo. Her mane of hair was just as wild and thick as Isac's unruly locks.

"Fortunately, its bleach blond and not pure silver," Karen joked.

Alice, on the other hand, had her mother's looks, with eyes of emerald ponds. Tom knew he would have his hands full fighting off the many suitors that were to come as she grew older.

On the first night of their weekend excursion, the family walked along the beach after dinner. Tom and Karen casually strolled hand in hand as the kids ran ahead to collect seashells.

"It's so good to get away," Karen said with a sigh of relief, "even just for two days. Both of us have needed this *little break*. We need to do this more often. Sometimes life can become so hectic with work, the kids' schooling, and Isac's afterschool activities that we forget to the *take time to smell the roses and appreciate all we have*."

Tom agreed. "You're right. Let's rebook for next month before we leave. I didn't realise how much I needed this time away together."

After a long, hard year, a little *rest and recreation* was just what they all needed. The couple sometimes found it hard to minimise their tunnel vision on work and prioritise the family. But their small family was the most important thing to them; the weekend away made them remember that.

On the drive home, Tom felt *pleased with himself*, and he knew Karen felt the same. They were both so grateful for how far they had come; even the kids seemed happier. It was great to have some time away to *have fun, let their hair down*, and *relax*. But with the end of their weekend trip, Karen and Tom's thoughts were back at the store, but this time with a *renewed* sense of pride and promise. Tom often dreamed of a time in the not-too-distant future where he was financially free and could afford to spend more quality time with his family.

When they arrived back home and unpacked, Karen and Tom sat outside with a cold beer. Suddenly, Tom thought of an idea to hold an appreciation party for all his suppliers and customers.

"We could also have a sale at the store to celebrate our first year. I could run an advert in the local paper offering a discount on all tools for the following Saturday, and I can even bring in our barbeque and offer a free sausage sandwich to whoever shows," he told Karen

She thought it was a great idea, and with that, they were back to planning. Just like before, everything fell into place without a hitch. When Karen told the local butcher and baker what they were planning at the store, they offered them a discount on the sausages and bread. Tom and Karen were once again blown away by the support their town had shown their little business, and they wanted to let them know just how much they were appreciated.

Keywords/Phrases: Stability, time to celebrate, happy family life, stable environment, great team, gratitude, rest and recreation, job complete, pleased, fun, relax, let your hair down.

Further Interpretations: Buying and selling property, important events (marriage), happy news arrives, rejoicing after hard work, celebrating achievements, pleasure, harmony.

Visual Representation: The Four of Wands represents a successful outcome for Tom and Karen's business. This is the time for them to show gratitude for what has been achieved and enjoy the fruits of their labour. Things are going well, and life is good. This card signifies that it's time to celebrate your achievements. With the stable, centred feeling the Four of Wands brings, the moment is right for reunions with family and friends. There is so much to be happy about. This card represents stability and the ability to stand erect and be proud of what you have accomplished thus far.

Five of Wands

Breaking into their third year of business, the store was continuing to operate quite nicely, and life was good in their house of ambition and drive. But little did Tom and Karen know, they were about to experience their first real *challenge*.

When they arrived at the store to open up one morning, they found a brochure slipped under the door advertising a new store that would open in their area at the end of the month. They were surprised to learn the new store would be much like their own in terms of inventory. It was a large franchised store that would offer many more products at a lower price and lower quality. Even though Tom knew his stock was of a higher quality, he was still worried. For the first time, he was faced with a bit of *competition*. Up until that point, he had singlehandedly held the market for all the local mechanics and repair stores.

In the days following the discovery of the new store, the atmosphere in the shop started to become heavy, and *quarrels and arguments* began breaking out more frequently. Tom and Karen felt the strain and stress of what was happening around them, and pent-up feelings of frustration began to surface. With the slight breakdown of leadership, the store's two employees began to handle situations in their own way, and the store quickly became unzipped. Everyone felt the pressure of working on a different page. Karen and Tom could not seem to see eye to eye on anything, and that *tension* led to even more disagreements in their relationship both at work and at home. Tom felt like he was losing control. Where once there was peace and calm, there was now *chaos*.

Some couples thrive off of a fiery relationship and use arguments and struggles to keep the relationship interesting, but Tom and Karen's behaviour was unbecoming and not like them at all. They both knew deep down that they needed to keep their tempers under control and listen to one another, as they were both fighting for the same cause. They had to understand that sales was a cutthroat industry, and they would have to fight to have their slice of success. Nothing about it was going to be easy.

"If you want it bad enough, go fight for it," Tom could hear his gran saying.

Many of Tom's friends dropped by to offer their opinions on what to do. It was clear he needed to *change* a few things to continue to stand out from the crowd and keep his clients, but it was a *challenging time* for all. Mundane matters began to go wrong, and more attention needed to be paid to securing suppliers.

About a week after hearing the news of the new store, Tom retired to his office and asked Karen for the phone numbers of all his suppliers. He started ringing around town to see where their loyalties lied. He found out that some of his suppliers would be supplying the new store as well as his own. Tom kept his cool and did not allow his ego to take over.

"Change is good," he told Karen. "Gran always said, 'Everything happens for a reason.'"

Once again, Tom began to think of what his gran would do or say in this situation, and in the back of his mind, he heard her say, "Do not dwell on the negative because what you think about you bring about." Whenever Tom was worried as a child, Gran would tell him that everything always works out and he should keep his mind on only the good things in life. Tom knew Gran was always right, so that night, he made a plan with Karen to start changing the way they thought about the situation.

"Let's stay positive!" he said.

He decided to *withdraw from the drama* because he knew deep down that everything would work out; it always did. *Healthy competition* made Tom stronger and even more positive that his store was the best. At all times, he kept his ethics high. He refused to buy into all the what-ifs. He told Karen to not think of competition as a bad thing. Surely, there was enough room in the area for two spare part stores.

Tom told his staff that their service and reasonable prices would keep their customers and that their jobs were secure. He was confident he had a lot more to offer than the new franchised store. A family business in a small town is what people want, and if Tom could keep his prices competitive, he would be able to keep the store growing. He was more than *ready to fight* because he believed in his store. There was no point in being defensive and territorial; that behaviour would get him nowhere fast.

Keywords/Phrase: Rivalry, challenges, obstacles, a need to fight, need for control, opposition, conflict, change your approach, stand out from the crowd, healthy competition, quarrels and arguments, tension, chaos, challenging time, withdraw from drama.

Further Interpretations: Self-doubt, bad vibes, a challenge erupts, honour, differences, release your ego.

Visual Representation: The Five of Wands has brought about challenges for Tom and Karen. Life cannot always be peaches and cream. It is how you handle yourself in times of conflict that matter most. Tom stood his ground in the face of struggle. He knew that if he changed the way he looked at his situation, it would change for the better, so he withdrew from all the drama and released his ego. He showed patience and had faith that everything would work out. Tom did what he could to overcome his obstacles.

Six of Wands

Tom arrived at the store early one icy morning and collected the mail from under the door. He tossed it on the office desk for Karen to open when she arrived later that morning after dropping the kids at school. Tom went about his business and was busy serving a customer when, just after lunch, Karen sprung from inside the office, shouting, "We won, *we won!*"

Tom was perplexed and, honestly, uninterested.

"What did we win?" he asked, giving Karen a look.

She jumped up and down and ran around the store in front of the customers.

"The best store in town!" Karen said, beaming. Little did Tom and Karen know, their store had been entered into a local business competition for best service to the area. "The best store!" Karen shouted again. She dramatically cleared her throat to read the notice out loud.

"Congratulations, T & K Spares! You have been named the winner of Best Store in this year's Chamber of Commerce Small Business competition. Your store was secretly judged on customer service, ability to supply customers' needs, friendliness, and your benefits to the local area."

Karen was thrilled, and although Tom was also happy, he was a little embarrassed because his customers were witnessing Karen's freak-out. Tom's customer shook his hand, *congratulated* him, and smiled over at Karen, who was slowly coming down from her enthusiastic outburst.

A full *award ceremony* was planned for the coming Saturday night to *celebrate their success,* and they were to be the *guests of honour.* Karen left Tom to finish serving his customer and immediately jumped on the phone to call her parents and tell them the good news. She was so proud of Tom. He had done a brilliant job making the store a community staple. *All the long hours, hard work, dedication, and commitment had finally paid off.*

The next day, a reporter and camera crew arrived at the store to do a feature story on T & K Spares for the local newspaper. It seemed as if Tom and Karen became *victorious, local celebrities* overnight.

The following Friday morning, before dropping the kids at school, Karen stopped by the local newsstand to pick up a few copies of the paper. She was stunned to see that her and Tom's article was on the front page. Everyone she saw that morning at the children's school stopped and congratulated her, and she was so humbled by their *best wishes.*

"What a great town we live in!" Karen said to Tom when she arrived at the store later that morning.

During a break between servicing customers and unpacking deliveries, Karen read Tom the news article.

"Huge congratulations go to T & K Spares for winning this year's Best Store award. T & K Spares has been operating for five years and is owned and operated by Tom and Karen Holmes. Tom was previously head mechanic at Maven's Garage for ten years before opening T & K Spares. Tom said he had a vision he just couldn't shake. He knew how risky and

challenging starting a new business would be after watching his parents work tirelessly on their own business before retiring, but he also knew it was something he was called to do. With the support from his wife Karen, who works alongside him full-time, both are able to successfully run the business and be loving parents to their two young children, Isac, 13, and Alice, 9.

"T & K Spares supplies the local area and beyond with mechanical parts. Tom said his experience working as a mechanic with the same tools he sells has given him valuable knowledge about what to stock and how to effectively help his customers. Tom and Karen's happy, warm personalities are what their customers comment on the most. Tom's former employer, Tony Marvin, owner of Marvin's Garage, had nothing but *admiration* and best wishes for Tom and Karen. He was thrilled when he heard the news that they had won this year's award."

The article went on to mention the award ceremony and wish T & K Spares all the *success* for its future.

"Isac and Alice will be thrilled to know they got a mention too," Karen said.

Keywords/Phrases: Winning, awards, public recognition, celebrate success, guest of honour, hard work and dedication have paid off, victorious, local celebrities, best wishes, huge congratulations, admiration.

Further Interpretations: Harmony, triumph, keep going, pride, victory in sight, on the right path, humility.

Visual Representation: With the Six of Wands, we can see Tom riding upon his horse full of pride and humility. Tom and Karen are great role models for their children and others. Winning an award was tremendous news. They'd worked hard and put everything they had into their business. They found themselves filled with more success, support, and love. Others will be guided by them, for they had the ability to succeed where others had not. The Six of Wands offers them a chance to enjoy their time in the spotlight and feel gratitude for the recognition they've received. Now, they can carry their wands proudly and bask in the limelight of their success.

Seven of Wands

All work and no play was beginning to take its toll on Tom. He had been continuously burning the candle at both ends and was working way more hours than he and Karen would have liked.

"I feel like I'm constantly *under attack* from the *demands* of our customers and suppliers. The *pressure* is starting to bring me down," Tom told Karen in the office one day.

Karen knew that things must be bad if Tom was talking to her about them. He rarely showed any cracks, even to her.

Lately, Tom had felt the mounting presence of his *competitor's* store and was *struggling* to keep his store on top. He knew the marketplace didn't leave much room to sit down and cry. He had to work on making his store better but not at the expense of his health or ethics.

But all the pressure Tom was feeling was beginning to show through the cracks. On more than one occasion, Tom had accidently ordered the wrong part, and his customers were not happy about it. He had been so busy that he even forgot to order parts from his supplier one month. The businesses Tom supplied depended on a reliable source of parts for their customers. If they could not get the parts needed to repair their customers' vehicles, then the garage would quickly suffer and perhaps develop a bad reputation. *His competitors took advantage* of Tom's mistakes, and word around town was not very pleasing to hear. One of Karen's friends said her husband was thinking of taking his business elsewhere. She also heard that a few suppliers were looking elsewhere too. This was not good to hear, and Karen knew she would have to talk with Tom that night. The new store downtown was growing fast, and Karen knew things would spiral out of control quite quickly if Tom couldn't *pull himself together.*

Tom and Karen already had two employees working alongside them at the store. Both were hardworking young men that Tom found invaluable. But even with all the extra hands, Tom found it hard to *delegate the workload*, as he had always been a man to do everything himself. This was something his Pops taught him as a child. "If you want something done, don't wait around for others to do it; make it happen yourself," Pops would say. Tom was a smart man, and he knew it was time to *rethink his position*, *reclaim his sanity*, and keep his customers happy.

One evening, he asked the boys to stay after work, and together, they worked out a strategic plan to get the store *back in good standing*. Karen was impressed by Tom's patience and was so proud of him for *stepping up* and realizing that he could no longer continue with the way things were before. He had to learn to delegate, or the store would crumble.

The bulk of Tom and the boys' plan was focused on how to work more efficiently. Tom *stood his ground* during the process and was determined to get his store *back on track and persevere*. He apologised to Karen and his customers for his mistakes and explained that it wouldn't happen again. He *defended himself* to the name slayers and put the entire mess behind him.

Later that night, after Tom closed the store and made it home, Karen explained to him that he may have caused the mess himself by taking on too much.

"You really have been working too hard and putting in way too many hours," Karen said. "The children miss you; you are hardly home in time to sit with us for dinner. You rarely make it home before Alice has gone to bed. They miss you, and Isac needs you. He is maturing right before our eyes." Tom knew Karen was right and explained what he and the boys had planned. Tom was *up for the challenge* to win his customers back from the new competition, and he was determined to keep his store the best in town despite it all.

Keywords/Phrases: Under attack, demands, pressure, competition, struggles, take advantage, pull yourself together, delegate the workload, rethink your position, reclaim your sanity, back in good standing, step up, stand your ground, back on track, persevere, defend yourself, up for the challenge

Further Interpretations: Self-defence, someone is trying to pull the rug out from under you. Do not listen to others' opinions.

Visual Representation: The Seven of Wands brings challenging times and a chaotic, conflict-ridden atmosphere. Tom's achievements are being questioned. His ego is being attacked by outside forces. Tom is a wise man and knows that when in deep water, become a better swimmer. He must now rethink his position and not become involved in other people's chaotic actions. He must not allow himself to buy into the confusion. He is determined to stand his ground, reclaim his personal power, and defend himself and his store. He will survive.

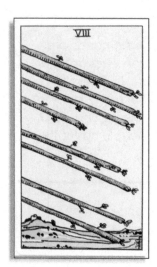

Eight of Wands

Life at the store settled down quickly after the period of confusion, and Tom was once again back on track mentally. He and his employees were finally working together as a team, and their early evening meeting had produced some great responses, with everyone now clear about their responsibilities. Tom had handed the job of ordering parts to one of the employees, and now he had more time to deal directly with his customers, which was the part of the job he loved the most. The store was *extremely busy*, and business was *cruising along* nicely. Tom had gained his confidence back in the face of adversity and felt like he was up for any new challenges. He was full of reclaimed power and *renewed energy*. He was thrilled when the store received an offer to supply a large mining operation with parts for their machines.

Karen and Tom jumped on the opportunity, *acting quickly.* They were over the moon on the inside but tried to remain grounded and not get carried away with what this new customer could mean for their store. They knew that supplying a mine with parts would bring many more challenges, but Tom felt it was time to *move forward, branch out, and expand their horizons.* His imagination ran unchecked at the possibilities, so Karen kept a watchful eye on him. After much deliberation, Tom and Karen decided to hire another employee to help at the store. Tom predicted he would have to spend quite a bit *of time traveling* to source parts. Karen was outwardly supportive, but Tom could tell she wanted him to remain cautious. She was excited about his newfound enthusiasm but tried to remain calm regardless.

After the anxieties and struggles of the past few months, Tom felt like his business was really *starting to grow.* All the difficulties the store had suffered were resolved, and everything was *expanding so quickly.* His supply was *in demand,* and he often had to travel away from home to source new suppliers. He and Karen knew they needed to strike while the iron was hot, but they missed each other immensely. Still, they understood the necessity of traveling at the moment. Tom called Karen every night he was away and talked with the kids, while Karen filled him in on how the store was doing. She reported that everything was fine and he had nothing to worry about. Karen knew that the time was right for Tom to be away to promote their business.

While she was happy about how everything turned out, Karen was relieved that the past few months of hardship were behind them. She was wise enough to understand that things often worsen before they improve. She knew that everyone and everything has a breaking point, and sometimes life will throw you a curveball just to shake things up. Often, restrictions and challenges make you appreciate the good in life.

Tom had learned from his past that it was important to be organised so things didn't spin out of control. He was doing well and was accepted by many new supply chains, which caused *business to soar.* Tom kept his focus and was *speeding forward with great momentum,* promoting his business any chance he could. *After struggling* with the new competition in town, Tom was a lot wiser as a businessman. Gran would have said, "Rejection is God's protection."

While Tom was away on business, Karen worked to rearrange the store so everything could run a little more fluidly. She also felt like it was a good time for a little promotion. Her head was full of *new inspirations and ideas,* like adding a line of workwear to the store. While Tom was away, she formed a plan to share with him when he returned. Karen ordered a few samples of work shirts, boots, and pants for both men and women. Times had changed, and just as many women were now working in the mining and mechanical fields. She was sure Tom would be impressed and see the added potential revenue this new line of products could bring to the store.

Keywords/Phrases: Busy, cruising along, renewed energy, acting quickly, move forward, branch out, expand your horizons, time traveling, starting to grow, in demand, soaring ahead, speeding forward, great momentum, after struggles, new inspiration & ideas.

Further Interpretations: Visitors coming from a distance, romance blossoms, and good news arrives, swiftness, evolutionary change.

> **Visual Representation:** Tom and Karen have come through the other side of the tough days, and this is a beautiful time. They feel no restrictions, and their life and business are both moving forward at a great pace. They are reaping the rewards of their hard work, and growth is assured. The sky is the limit for them. They must act fast on the good news that has come their way and make progress without letting obstacles block their path. Everything is moving so fast, which is shown with the Wands flying through the air. There's no time to waste. This is a card of swift action.

Nine of Wands

Tom had been away from home quiet a lot lately, traveling long distances. He arrived home from his most recent work trip *exhausted,* battered, bruised, and incredibly tired. He knew his work trips were important and valuable, but he began to feel a little defensive. Tom believed that he no longer needed to prove himself as a bona fide businessman. He had already achieved more than he thought possible. His shop was a huge success, and Karen's new line of workwear was a real hit. Tom was most impressed. His family was happy, but he knew he needed to endure the pains of the job and put in a *little more effort* and long hours before he could pass on the reins and retire.

Karen had noticed that, since Tom's return, her once happy-go-lucky, down-to-earth man had begun to act out of character and was displaying some erratic behaviours. Lately Tom had been testing everyone's patience. The smallest inconvenience would set him off. Last week, Karen arrived at work to find Tom yelling and ranting in the back of the store about something that Tom himself couldn't even explain. Tom was completely burnt out, and at that moment, he was *ready to throw it all away*. He simply could not go on working as he had been. His energy was all used up, and his strength had completely left him. But as the saying goes, "You can't hold a good man down," and *from somewhere, somehow,* Tom knew he would find the will and energy reserves he needed to *continue on* and see his business succeed. Karen knew her husband would fight on, so she asked the boys who worked at the store to stay out of Tom's way for a while until he was himself once again. They all had been feeling the pressure.

Before dinner one Friday night, Tom was sitting alone on the back porch with a cold beer when Karen joined him. She sat down on the warm concrete steps and put her arm over Tom's shoulders, resting her head on his with a deep sigh. She decided to gently approach the subject of Tom possibly slowing down on the work front. To her surprise, Tom listened without saying a word. When Karen had finished her spiel, Tom turned toward her, held her by the hands, and smiled.

"I know; you're right," Tom said. "I have been thinking the same thing. Tomorrow I am going to pass on more responsibilities to the boys. *I'm beat,* and I know *I cannot go on* working this way for much longer. Tomorrow I will make a few changes. I'm not ready to throw in the towel just yet; there is still life in this old boy," Tom said with a chuckle. Karen was stunned at his honesty and a little relieved. She expected some resistance from Tom but got none. They sat together in silence until the sun set below the hills as Tom finished his beer.

"Let's go in for dinner," Karen said, giving him a slight nudge.

The next day, Tom handed the job of managing the store to Paul, his longest-tenured employee. He would continue to travel and source the stock they needed, but when he was home, he would work in the store under more controlled hours. Tom knew this was *not the time to give up* completely, considering *how close* he was to reaching his dreams. He and Karen had built the store from the ground up and were living comfortably off its rewards. But Tom's new goal was to keep the store running smoothly without his or Karen's input. Karen was amazed at Tom's *determination, perseverance, and pure strength.* She was in awe of the man she married. They *were so close* to retiring, but Tom and Karen both knew they must *hang in there a little while longer* until their final goal of financial security could be reached.

Keywords/Phrases: Exhausted, little more effort needed, ready to throw it all away, from somewhere somehow, beat, cannot go on, not the time to give up, so close, determination, perseverance, pure strength, hang in there a little while longer, stay focused

Further Interpretations: One more obstacle or hiccup before success, end in sight, stay focused, a need for strong discipline, don't slacken off now, re-evaluate, think for yourself.

Visual Representation: Tom was so close to making it, but the pressure had become too much, and he found himself in a state of limbo. All nine wands were beginning to be quite heavy. Does he have the strength to push on, or should he chuck it all in? He had a lot to ponder, and he felt as if he was at a breaking point. But he is a man of determination and knows he should give it one more go and stick it out, if not for himself then for his family. The Nine of Wands tells us that complete success and happiness are not far away, so it's best to stick to the plan and carry on.

Ten of Wands

It didn't take too long for Tom to return to his old ways. Since arriving back at the store after being away for a week, he hit the ground running. "There's so much to do," he'd always say to Karen. All the *responsibilities* Tom gave the boys had slowly been reversed. He felt like he was the only one who could do the work. He found it hard to accept that others could do the job just as well, or even better, as he could. If he ever allowed one of the boys to take over a job for him, Tom would hover over their shoulder, checking to see if it was done right.

"I wonder why you feel so *burnt out*," Karen said to Tom one night. He had been feeling *more pressured and burdened* than ever. From working so hard and *carrying a heavy load*, he had lost all the enthusiasm he once had for the store. Tom had achieved everything he set out to do, yet at the end of it all, he was a sad man.

As time went on, the business became larger and harder to manage. The excitement and enthusiasm Tom had in the beginning had all but faded, and Karen was worried. As Tom walked through the door after a hard day, she sat him down for a long, overdue chat. She gave him permission to stop, hand over the store, and *lay down his burdens of responsibility*. The *hard* work and long hours Tom had put into his business over the many years had started to catch up with him, and his health was failing. Success has a price, and Karen explained that the fame, wealth, and power they've achieved with their business was nothing like what they expected when they first started. Tom had proved himself to her and himself.

Tom had fought hard to build a wonderful life for himself and his family, but he now felt like he was *carrying the weight of the world* on his shoulders. He realised that this burden was all of his own making. He clung tightly to everything he had built, only to find himself feeling *oppressed and exhausted* under the weight of it all. His passion for adventure and his willingness to take risks were lost; he was caught up in nothing but being the perfect, all-around man. Over the years, Tom had become president of the local football club Isac was a member of, maintained his role on the local council, and worked sixty hours a week at the store. Karen finally said *enough was enough*.

Karen convinced Tom to *share the load, slow down*, and enjoy the rest of his life. "We have enough; we will be fine," Karen said with pleading eyes. "It is time to start saying no more often and mean it."

Tom had a tendency of saying yes before realising the commitment involved. He had a soft heart, and if a friend ever asked him to lend a hand, Tom was always there to offer support. He would put whatever he had planned on the back burner to help another. Tom had always been a good listener, but this caused some people to assume that Tom was always available to be a psychological carrier for all their emotional baggage, *loading him up* with all their worries and fears.

"I'm sure some of the men that come into the store just come in for a chat," Karen said. "You always know what to say to make them feel better."

In that moment, his Gran would probably tell him he was

carrying too much *bad energy*, and Karen reminded him of this often. Although his big heart was something Karen admired about him, it was only a matter of time before he'd have to pay the price for being so kind-hearted. Now, he was paying dearly.

Keywords\Phrases: Responsibilities, burn out, pressured, burdened, carrying a heavy load, lay down your burden of responsibility, carrying the weight of the world, oppressed, exhausted, enough is enough, share the load, slow down, bad energy.

Further Interpretations: Taking on more than you can handle, stress, persistence is necessary, over-committed, declutter your life, make space.

Visual Representation: Tom is at his wit's end and feels he cannot go on any longer. The burden of all the business responsibilities has fallen on the couple's shoulders. Karen can sympathise with Tom to an extent, but she knows life would be much easier if they both laid down some of their burdens. As Gran would say, "Ask your angels to lighten the load." All the pressure from the Ten of Wands caused Tom to lose sight of the bigger picture. But tens not only represent the end but a new beginning, so Tom and Karen must find a way to balance their load, declutter their life and move on.

Page of Wands

After years of hard work, Tom and Karen were finally ready to retire. Tom was a classic and was able to pick himself up, dust himself off, and move on with ease. Sitting once again at his favourite spot on the back steps of their home, Tom thought back to his *early ideas* of opening a store, when he knew he was standing on *fertile ground* and his *dreams could be a possibility*, when everything was still in his head and not yet formulated. He remembered his *childlike passion* and was *full of enthusiasm* to begin his *new venture.* Back at the beginning of the dream, *and* his fearless free spirit, there were so many wonderful opportunities; the excitement was undeniable. Becoming his own boss was something he had wanted to do for a long time, but he never thought he was quite ready. Boy, was he wrong.

Tom was always *up for the challenge,* but his only regret was losing his *youthful optimism* along the way. Tom felt like he was now ready *to take up another challenge*, have a go with a *new creative adventure, and follow his passions* wherever they may take him. He knew what he needed and that his skills were still sharp. This time, though, he had come to this decision armed with wisdom and knowledge, knowing that a new stage of life was about to begin. Tom knew that when he was confident and happy in his skin, he would be able to achieve anything he put his mind to. He had every reason to feel confident, as everything he needed was at his disposal. He could *take action*, knowing he was ready to step into his power.

Keywords/Phrases: Early days, fertile ground, dreams becoming a reality, childlike passion, full of enthusiasm, new adventure, up for the challenge, fearless free-spirit, youthful optimism, creative adventures, follow your passion, take action

Further Interpretations: People-person, energetic, extravert, loves a challenge, brave, optimistic, certain, active, cocky, active kid, a messenger.

Further Interpretations: When Tom gets an idea or experiences life's great aha moments, he is hard to hold down. He has so much inner strength and passion and is full of creative ideas that are ready to be explored. New ideas constantly flood his mind, and as such, he is always thinking of the work that lies ahead. The Page of Wands illustrates the early days, when Tom's plans were just beginning to gather momentum.

KNIGHT of WANDS.

Knight of Wands

Tom had never been one to remain idle for long. His gran would say he was a firefly when he was a boy, always flitting in and out, *charging ahead* of everyone else. He was *confident, cocky, and ready* to carve out a *glorious adventure*. There was *no holding him back;* he was a bull at the gate. He was very *wilful*, and if he didn't get his way, he would act out in anger. He had the spirit of adventure deep within. So, whenever Tom had plans for a new endeavour, *all systems were a go.*

Even with his tenacity and take-the-bull-by-the-horns approach to life, Tom was also *intuitive.* He had the ability and imagination to take up a new idea long before anyone else caught on. Tom was *no follower*—never was, never will be; he was *an innovator, a trailblazer, a trendsetter.* When Tom felt like it was *time for action*, he *acted quickly.* He'd start putting all his plans into motion with excitement and optimism.

Although Tom was *ready for the adventure* of a lifetime, he thought about *his plan carefully.* Sure, he had a tendency to *act quickly and, at times, make rash decisions.* He was full of immense self-confidence, but wisdom was required too. Over the years, he had mastered the *art of endurance, stamina, and speed,* but Tom remembered what his gran once said: "Life is not a sprint. Remain true to yourself. What is yours will never pass you by. Listen to the call of your soul, for it will never lead you astray."

Keywords/Phrases: Charging ahead, confident, ready, no holding back, spirit of adventure, wilful, all systems go, intuitive, not a follower, innovative, trailblazer, trendsetter, time for action, acts quickly, can be rash, endurance, stamina, speed

Further Interpretations: Lusty, free-spirited, competitive, hot-blooded, charismatic, loyal, change of residence, materialisation of the impossible happening, impulsive, deeply passionate, inspired creativity.

Visual Representation: Tom has moved past the thinking phase of the Page and into the action phase. He is rearing at the bit, ready to charge full steam ahead. Gran was so right when she called him a firefly. Tom was a hard man to hold back. He faced most of life's challenges head on. He was always willing to get the job done and would not hesitate to bowl you over if you stood in his way. Tom loved the saying, "Action speaks louder than words" and would preach it to Isac and Alice a lot. He told them his pops instilled those traits in him as a child, and he hoped Isac and Alice would heed his advice.

Queen of Wands

It never really occurred to Tom just how lucky he had been in life, with his delightful family, incredible wife who adored him, and the wise teachings from Gran. No matter the circumstances, he was always able to accomplish his goals, and with Karen by his side, he felt like *anything was possible.* Karen was *independent* and loved Tom immensely. She was *a hard worker* in her own right—*capable, empathic, and adventurous.* She would remain forever *loyal* in her marriage with Tom. Tom was also very *well-liked*, and people tended to flock to him because of his *charisma.* Both Tom and Karen were extremely friendly, warm, and passionate. They possessed a down-to-earth charm that others really admired. Both had a way of easily balancing their work and family life. Karen had always said that they were alike in so many ways. Tom possessed many feminine traits and was *passionate, charming, practical,* and liked by many. Against Karen's innate masculine qualities, they were both *capable leaders,* though they had a tendency to be *impulsive* at times.

Over the years, Tom had matured and was more *in tune* with his hunches, or his *"intuition"* as his gran would call it. He had the energy of a thinker, a *creator.* In fact, Tom created every day via his thoughts, feelings, intentions, and actions. Flashes of inspiration gave rise to great success. Tom was inspired to *follow his heart, listen to his head, and act.* When

Tom got an idea, he believed he could see it through, so *he applied himself* and kept going until he *reached the fruition of his dreams*. He had every reason to be optimistic. As Gran would say, "Always remember that you are divinely protected and divinely directed."

Keywords/Phrases: Hard worker, capable, empathic, adventurous, loyal, well-liked, charismatic, passionate, charming, practical, born leader, impulsive, in tune, initiative, creative, follow your heart, listen to your head, apply yourself, follow your dreams.

Further Interpretations: Feisty, self-assured, good businessperson, good communicator, warm, passionate, knows their value.

Visual Representation: Karen and Tom are doers, forever full of creative energy. They prefer to get in there and get their hands dirty instead of sitting on the sidelines watching. They are both immensely capable and have the added knack of being able to balance home and work life, Karen more so than Tom at times. They are both born leaders and are capable of just about anything they set their minds to. Both of them excel in business and are great communicators. They both know their value and are always warm, passionate, and caring.

King of Wands

Tom had gained a lot of experience over his lifetime and had become someone who *takes control*. He liked being his own *boss* and, as one, would never expect anyone to do more than him. He was a *fair but firm leader, magnetic, and determined*. He was also very well *respected* by his staff and customers. Tom had a genuine concern for others, which easily motivated him to do the work he did. When you were an employee of his, you worked with him, not for Tom. Though he had a caring and understanding side, he was also *very direct, to the point, and honest*. He didn't mess around. There was no fluff with him. People always knew where they stood with Tom.

Tom was destined to be a *business owner*. This was his calling. He had always *been honest, positive, forthright,* and ready to *take on new challenges*. He wasn't one to sit and watch others; Tom was *a leader*. Over the years, Tom had developed *patience,* which was something he lacked in his younger days. He was now more *self-disciplined* and *a straight shooter*. When Tom knew what he wanted, he did not remain idle; he preferred to *act on impulse*.

Karen noticed that Tom had a tremendously *infectious spirit of fiery energy*. He was enthusiastic, but he was not a brash man; he was a *strategist*. He naturally developed his vision and imagination and wasn't afraid to use his power to manifest them. His warm, *infectious personality* constantly convinced others to follow his lead. Karen noticed that Tom has an *intolerance for ignorance* and at times was certain he was right, even if someone showed him facts that proved he wasn't. He was unquestionably a *sore loser* and could become overbearing if things didn't go his way.

As they say, no one can have it all.

Keywords/Phrases: Takes control, fair, firm, leader, magnetic, determined, respected, very direct, to the point, honest, business owner, positive, forthright, take up challenges, patient, self-disciplined, straight shooter, acts on impulse, infectious spirit, fiery energy, intolerant to ignorance, sore loser.

Further Interpretations: Mature, competitive, good-hearted, kind, inspirational, driven, dramatic, courageous, handy man, problem solver, good friend.

Visual Representation: Tom is a great man and a confident leader. He is well-liked by all who know him. He is a problem solver and will not rest until he gets it right. He exudes control and authority, but he does so with charm and poise. He is genuinely concerned about the welfare of others. Tom confidently sits on his throne, secure in his position as an exceptional business owner.

II

THE PENTACLES

THE
PENTACLES

"TRY NOT TO BECOME A MAN OF SUCCESS,
BUT RATHER A MAN OF VALUE."
— ALBERT EINSTEIN

The Pentacles cover the mundane, material aspects of life, including property, money, home, nature, manifestation, realisation, proof, and prosperity. This suit is associated with matters of security, stability, and wealth. The Pentacles are connected to the element of earth; therefore, they are realistic, secure, and growth-oriented in nature. Earth is where seeds are sown and where we stand firm. As such, the Pentacles relate to all things that will stand the test of time.

Ace of Pentacles

After many years of dedication and hard work, the time had come for Tom and Karen to sell their store. They were ready to start a new chapter in their lives. Selling the store was not an easy decision, but they both knew it was the right one to make. Tom and Karen had made many sacrifices over the years to see their business grow and be the success it now was. Together, they were ready to expand and see what the universe had in store for them and their future.

Karen advertised their business online, and within a day, they received inquiries. The phone was running hot. Tom barely had time for a break before the phone rang once again. He was amazed at the offers they received, as several were well over the asking price. Their business was in hot demand. Recently, a real estate friend told Tom that the goodwill they have generated over the years was worth quite a bit of money in today's market. He seemed to be right because the phone never stopped ringing with inquiries from all over the state.

Karen spent a great deal of her time the following week emailing their business profile and financials to prospective buyers. The couple had prospered well over the years, and the store had been very good to them financially. The books looked promising for any new owner, and it seemed as if the store had *huge potential* for further *growth,* which Tom explained well to prospective buyers, adding his vision of how he saw the store progressing in the future. He also told prospective buyers about the growth of the nearby mine and the extra revenue this could attract.

With the sale of their business, Tom and Karen would have more than *enough money available* for Isac and Alice's education as well as a comfortable future. All their hard work, effort, and commitment were about to pay off, and they would be well compensated for it. The years at the store had brought forth the couple's faith in their abilities, and they were now ready put it to use and further themselves in the world. The wealth coming from the sale of the store wasn't the only perk; in addition, Tom would now have more time to finish all the jobs around the house that he had been putting off for years.

With all the interest the store generated, Tom thought the *time was right* to make an appointment with the bank and discuss his and Karen's financial future. Karen was thinking about *building a new home*, and Tom was certain *their possibilities were endless.* They had been tied to their store for so long that they had forgotten what living was all about. With the store sold, they would be free from the shackles of long hours and no holidays off and could at long last reclaim precious time with their children.

After Tom visited with his bank manager, financial advisor, and accountant, he was happy to report to Karen that all the extra money they had invested in their superannuation had grown considerably over the years. They were much *wealthier than they expected,* and a newly built home was definitely a possibility. The sky was the limit, *the opportunities were endless,* and Karen and Tom were open and ready for whatever the universe brought their way.

Sometimes, there are times in life when, out of the blue, *you feel blessed* in ways that are difficult to explain. Karen recognized that this was one of those rare moments. The *windows of opportunity were open wide,* and the couple were excited to see where it led them. This was a very *auspicious and fortunate time* in their lives. The *funds would be available* to further any endeavours they wished to undertake. Life was good, and Karen and Tom began to make plans for their future.

Keyword/Phases: Huge potential, growth, enough money made available, timing was right, new home, possibilities are endless, extra money, wealthier than expected, endless opportunities, feeling blessed, auspicious and fortunate time, funds available.

Further Interpretations: Healing and clarity, manifest your dreams, a win, a promotion, good investments, new income, new offer leads to security, abundance, organised, centred, manifestation.

Visual Representation: The hand of opportunity pictured on the Ace of Pentacles is offering Tom abundance. The garden path is clear to explore endless possibilities. This is a great time in Karen and Tom's life. All their funds are available for them to pursue any new adventure they have their hearts set on. The opportunities are unlimited. They are full of fresh energy and inspiration for what lies ahead in the future. The Ace of Pentacles represents great wealth and happiness. This new-found happiness could be the result of something that's been in the making for a while. The wealth this card offers, however, does not need to be monetary. Enjoying time with family is one of the greatest gifts of life that cannot be bought. Still, financial abundance is available for Tom and Karen to enjoy life and explore new investments.

Two of Pentacles

After Tom returned from the bank, he sat down with Karen to discuss their plans. After the dinner dishes were put away, both Isac and Alice went out to visit with friends, so the house was quiet. Tom carefully listened, sipping his coffee, as Karen explained what she had in mind for their future. In the middle of her sentence, she grabbed a box from the other room and placed all their financial records on the table, which included a mass of books and folders in every colour. Tom was unsurprised, as he knew Karen was a diligent bookkeeper. It seemed to Tom that Karen had kept a record of every transaction the store had ever made. Karen explained that these figures on those pages were only from the previous two years, but she could produce more if needed. Tom refused and admitted that he had never really had a head for numbers.

"That's why I married you," he joked. Karen gave him a sly look that made Tom smile.

They spent the next few hours poring over their books and putting together a *budget* they were both happy with. They considered rising interest rates and the struggling economy when they set their new asking price for the store. They worked tirelessly into the night to come up with a plan that would allow them to afford a new home and still have money for their kids' education. They made sure they set aside enough money to enjoy their future comfortably. It would be tight in some areas, but they decided on a *perfect balance* that left everyone happy, even their bank manager. They knew there was a fine line between feast and famine, having rode the waves of small business for years.

They were both strong believers in the phrase "*money makes money,*" and they understood that it may be necessary to take a small *risk* and use some of the capital from the sale of their business to build a larger nest egg for their future. They had already put some money aside, as they preferred to not tie it all up so money was available when needed. They *juggled their finances* carefully, trying to avoid taking from Peter to pay Paul. They didn't want to *leave themselves short.*

"Building a new home has a way of blowing out the budget real quick," Tom informed Karen.

Both Karen and Tom knew they must *remain flexible* during this time. Life, up to that point, had become quite rigid, as if they had been living Groundhog's Day over and over for many years. They were careful to find a *happy balance.* They had become content with the pattern of their everyday lives, but they were also looking forward to branching out to *new horizons.* Still, they desired to stay stress-free by *managing* their *finances* carefully and *making decisions* slowly and logically.

Change would do them both good; they both agreed on that. Even if they were not sure exactly where the next chapter of their life would lead, they stayed optimistic. The *energy and money* would be *available;* that was the main thing. They both had faith that life would present them with the perfect people at the perfect time who were ready to step into an extraordinary opportunity and make miracles happen.

"If she was here right now, Gran would say to just go with the flow and know that everything will be OK," Tom said.

Karen agreed wholeheartedly, so they packed away their

books and headed off to bed knowing that all was well and their future looked bright.

Keywords/Phrases: Budget, perfect balance, money makes money, risks, juggling your finances, don't leave yourself short, remain flexible, making decisions, change, happy balance, new horizons, energy and money available.

Further Interpretations: Juggling different aspects of their life, decisions that must be made, changes and fluctuations, ups and downs in money matters, keep the balance, remain adaptable, fancy footwork.

Visual Representation: Tom and Karen have arrived at an important part of their lives. If the Ace of Pentacles represented the beginning of a new business or financial venture, the Two of Pentacles represents the need to balance that venture with other important areas of life, such as family, friends, and even our own physical, mental, and spiritual well-being. There are many decisions to make. Finding a way to effectively juggle their finances can ensure that the couple's future is successful and happy after the sale of their business. At this time, Karen and Tom are experiencing vast changes and fluctuations, so they need to be particularly careful about balancing their skills when they plan for the future.

Three of Pentacles

For now, Karen and Tom borrowed against their existing home to obtain a home loan so work could begin on their new house. They purchased a large block of land on the outskirts of town a few years back when the property market crashed, a true steal. Karen knew one day she would have the chance to build her dream home, and that time had finally come. Tom and Karen put together a *great team* of builders and architects to help make their dream a reality, and the plans were sent off to the local council for approval. The couple appreciated the expertise, feedback, and direction their builders offered them. They were hopeful that everyone *could pull all their resources together and collaborate in harmony.* Tom and his builders formed a *formidable team,* and Karen said that she was convinced their new house was going to be a masterpiece.

The new build was Karen's dream come true. She loved helping the team create the décor, and she had a real flare for design. Karen also *loved working as part of a team* where everyone felt comfortable sharing their ideas. Days on the building site were exciting, and their new house was the talk of the town. Tom had also received an offer to buy the house upon completion at a considerable profit, but Karen refused.

"We are building something of lasting worth," she told Tom. "This is something we can leave the kids when the time comes." Tom was never really thinking of selling, but he thought Karen should be aware of the attention their home was creating.

Over the next couple weeks, their house's structure was coming along nicely. Karen organised a working bee one Sunday morning to help with the landscaping. Many of their friends came over to lend a hand. Tom fired up the barbeque and put on a few sausages so everyone could have a sandwich. Beers were flowing, and before long, their yard had begun to take shape. Everyone *contributed their skills,* from digging to planting to pushing the barrow full of compost. Even the kids joined in. Everyone had a great day, and Tom and Karen fell even more in love with their *community of like-minded friends* and family.

Tom knew little about gardening but learned a lot from his more earthy friends. He was a patient and observant student and knew when to ask for guidance. Karen, on the other hand, loved gardening and was in her element. The house was coming together, and both Karen and Tom loved it. They still had a long way to go, but the builders worked tirelessly. Tom knew when to step back and let the experts in, and he was in awe of the work that had been carried out so far. He told Karen that he was sure Gran brought everyone together. She was always one to say that many hands made light work.

That night as Tom climbed into bed feeling exhausted but happy, Karen leaned over and kissed him.

"What an awesome day," she said. "There is something very satisfying about *everyone working together on the same page.* Did you notice how everyone had times when they would lead and others followed and vice versa? Everyone got on so well. There was a real kinship, and I could feel that everyone felt they had a purpose and were appreciated. You know, Tom, there is no greater feeling of accomplishment than knowing you have a purpose," she said as she switched off the light.

Keywords/Phrases: Pull your resources together, calibrate in harmony, formidable team, everyone working together, contribution of skills, community, like-minded friends, everyone working together, on the same page, teamwork.

Further Interpretations: Collaborations, paid for being creative, rewards, artistic endeavours, participation, allies, focused intention.

Visual Representation: With the Three of Pentacles, Tom and Karen have found fulfilment and are in the process of manifesting their new home. Their inspiration is becoming concrete in the material world, and they've successfully made big decisions. They now have the space to enjoy some initial satisfaction, and their joint project is well underway. However, the Three of Pentacles does not indicate the final completion; rather this is just the beginning. The project will invite others to help and will serve as the manifestation of a creative union.

Four of Pentacles

At last Tom and Karen received a serious offer from a prospective buyer who wished to purchase their store. All of a sudden, Tom began to have second thoughts and was reluctant to sell. It was all beginning to get too real for his liking. For many years, Tom had worked hard to build the store to the success it was today. His work had been fruitful, and *possessiveness* gripped him. Tom held on tightly and would not budge on his price. If he was going to sell his business, he wanted to be more than compensated for the years he had put in, but at the same time, he felt like a little piece of who he was would be lost along with the store itself. He had a *great fear of loss but holding on* would end up *stagnating* his creative flow of energy. Sooner or later, he would have to *allow for change.* Karen tried her best to make him see sense, but he wouldn't listen.

Tom was *stuck* in the *mindset of lack,* and from there, he would only welcome more lack and *hardship* into his life if he did not let go. He needed to trust that everything would work out. A brief time of instability allowed for a continuous flow of wealth to come toward him. But Tom was not listening, even though he knew his gran would say the same things as Karen. He just couldn't let go. He told Karen that the store had been good to them for years, and they had led a very stable life. He was *afraid of change* and worried about the future.

Karen explained that his tight grasp was *stopping his flow of energy,* and for the flood gates to open, they had to let go of the familiar. She reminded him of what his gran would say. She knew he was struggling with his self-confidence and *insecurities,* but she assured him that the fear of letting go could result in *not only material but emotional stagnation* as well.

"Letting emotional energy flow goes hand in hand with letting material resources flow. Holding on will *create internal as well as external blockages.* Take the risk and let's move on," Karen said. "Where one door closes, another opens. The fear of loss can mean no loss, but it also can mean no gain either. I know you have your fears and doubts; that is natural, but it is time, Tom. Let it go."

Tom knew Karen was right, but he still clung on tightly. Karen decided to drop the subject for a while, hoping Tom would see the light and the buyer would hang around.

Karen remained silent for a few days, but the frustration she felt from Tom's stubbornness began to creep under her skin. She waited until the kids were out of the house to broach the subject with Tom once again. After dinner, while Tom rested and read the local paper, Karen sat beside him and took his hand in hers. Tom put down his paper, knowing what was on Karen's mind. He had been trying to avoid the conversation for days, but he knew Karen would not let this rest.

Tom had always been tight with money, never wanting to spend it on anything meaningless. Karen once bought a new bedroom set, and Tom almost had a breakdown. "What was wrong with the old one?" he had asked. "We have had it all our married life, and I wanted a change," Karen replied. Tom just shook his head and sulked away. Even though Karen handled all the books at the store and looked after their household bills, Tom always knew where they stood financially. Karen explained that, with the sale, they would have enough to pay off their new house and have ample left over to invest. Tom listened closely, and when Karen finished putting up a good case, even pulling out the big guns by saying how disappointed his Gran would be in his behaviour, Tom held up his hand to stop Karen from going any further and told her he would think about it.

Keywords/Phrases: Possessiveness, great fear of loss, stagnation, stuck, mindset of lack, hardship, afraid of change, stopping the flow of energy, insecurities, material and emotional stagnation, internal and external blockages

Further Interpretations: Nothing ventured and nothing gained, holding back, not joining in, give and receive, saving for a rainy day, protect your resources.

Visual Representation: The Four of Pentacles is the card of the miser. The man on the card has one pentacle on his head, which represents that his thoughts are all about his "stuff." He has one in his arms, indicating that he is not free to do anything else. And he also can't go anywhere because his feet are busy holding the remaining two coins down. In other words, this man is so tied up with his possessions that he can't do anything else. His possessions are his life. This is where Tom is standing.

Five of Pentacles

Weeks passed, and not much had changed. Karen was beginning to become a little concerned about Tom's narrow-mindedness and possessiveness of the store. The new store in town was still doing well, and Tom was finding it hard to adjust to the challenges of competition. On most days, he rambled about how his store was there first and so on. His employees were becoming tired of hearing him complain. Even his customers sensed that the store had lost its energy, and some had taken their business elsewhere. The passion Tom once felt had begun to vanish once again.

With his constant negativity, Tom was beginning to *lose money,* and his business was *suffering* badly. Karen sadly informed Tom that their store just barely broke even the past month, and if he didn't do something soon, they might lose the whole business and their new house. Tom was in denial and was entering a period of *mental scarcity and hardship,* something he knew Karen forewarned months ago. Tom was beginning to lose faith in himself, and he found himself withdrawing, not even talking to Karen about *how cast out* he felt. He knew deep down he had brought the collapse upon himself. His stubbornness and narrow focus caused him to miss an opportunity to sell when he had great offers. Each day, Tom drove by the new store after work to take a look. He was too afraid to get out of the car and go in to witness for himself what was going on. He felt *disconnected* from everything around him, even Karen.

Loss and failure gripped him hard, and Tom knew he had to control his negative self-talk. His Gran would always tell him to look on the bright side and always search for the good in everything, but Tom had all but given up hope of saving his store, and his marriage was suffering as well. The *misery outside* is only a reflection of the *misery inside,* and with each passing day, Tom became more and more *despondent.* Tom wondered if he should seek help from a counsellor, but he didn't want to upset Karen or hear "I told you so." "Negative thoughts can create self-fulfilling prophecies," Gran often said. "If you want to change the world, you must first change yourself." He held out hope that, somehow, he would make his way through this *difficult time.*

Tom had seen the light and was well aware that he should have listened to Karen and sold the store when they were doing well and the offers were better. Hanging on had caused his demise. He confused his self-worth with his material security and felt his sense of direction and faith in himself had left. Tom had even been reluctant to watch Isac play football on the weekend, which was something he never missed. Karen always told him he was his own worst enemy, and he was beginning to think she was right.

Tom finally admitted defeat to Karen when he got home from work one Friday night. "You were right; we should have sold sooner," Tom said as he sat at the table. "Do you think it is too late to try again? The previous people who showed interest in the store might still be interested. I think I will contact them tomorrow; you just never know. Gran would say, 'Fail fast and learn from defeat, then keep going. Know when to fold your cards.'" Tom dropped his head in shame.

Forever the optimist, Karen placed her hand on Tom's

cheek and said, "We will get through this together, Tom. Everything will work out; you'll see."

Keywords/Phrases: Financial loss, suffering, mental scarcity, hardship, cast out, disconnected, loss and failure, misery, despondent, difficult times.

Further Interpretations: Poverty, worry, isolation, spiritual bankruptcy, change habits, setbacks, unemployment, loss in faith, fear, lack, rumination.

Visual Representation: The Five of Pentacles not only represents a time of financial strife but a time of despair and loneliness. Just as the Four of Pentacles indicates a psychological attachment to money and a tendency to overvalue the means of exchange, the Five of Pentacles is also likely to indicate an inner difficulty with your relationship to money and material things. In the story, Tom suffers from a lack of confidence, which is reflected in his self-judgment. When money becomes the primary motivating force in life and the gauge by which we judge our worth, a lack of it may produce anxiety and a sense of being excluded from the good things money can provide. Although Tom has encountered financial difficulties, he must beware of falling into the trap of losing faith in his ability so he can recreate a positive financial situation for himself and his family.

Six of Pentacles

After much deliberation, poking and listening to common sense from Karen, Tom at last relinquished control and once again placed the store up for sale. It didn't take long for a substantial offer to come in, and the couple quickly accepted. Tom was relieved and at peace with his decision. He took Karen out to lunch, and they ordered some champagne to celebrate.

"What an ordeal," he said. He was confident that he was being *well compensated* for all his hard efforts. He and Karen were now financially secure, and their future would be well taken care off. They paid off their new home, which only came in a little over budget, definitely not as bad as Tom expected. Their store sold for *much more than they both anticipated,* which also helped. Tom offered a *generous bonus* to each of his staff members for their loyalty and support over the years before he left. Tom and Karen were so *grateful* for their alliance and faith when life at the store was tough. Fortunately, the new owners were keeping Tom's employees on, which he encouraged.

Tom's *act of kindness* went a long way. To Tom and Karen's surprise, their employees held a small party to honour them both and celebrate their years of dedication to the store. Everyone felt a little sad about their departure, and they wanted to say a fond farewell on their last day together. Friends, their suppliers, and many of their customers dropped in to wish them well. Tom and Karen would be missed, and everyone was sad to see them go. Before everyone left, one of Tom and Karen's loyal employees stood on the counter to make a toast in honour of their favourite bosses. Everyone raised their glasses and wished them the best for their future. Karen struggled to hold back her tears. She knew her and Tom had made the right decision, but she felt a sense of loss all the same.

Tom at last had *renewed faith* in his future, and Karen was happy to have her old Tom back. When everything looked like it was going belly up and they were about to face a huge loss, *good fortune* crossed their path at the last minute. Gran smiled down from above once again. Offers of employment for both Tom and Karen were well received, but both were looking forward to a small rest, for the time being anyway. Tom had immense gratitude for everything in his life and had learned to *give and receive* with grace, *to be generous* and also *accept generosity in return.*

Now that the store sale was finalized, Karen's parents brought up her and Tom's plans for the future. Many people in town were watching and waiting to see where they would go, knowing that Tom was a restless man and would not remain idle for long. Karen assured her parents that they were both happy and just wanted to see where life would take them. They were at last financially secure and ready for a new chapter in their life to begin.

The difficult period was now behind them, and both Tom and Karen were once again at peace with one another. Their future looked bright because they both trusted the process of *change and growth.* There was a great sense of freedom after being tied to the store for years. They planned a little getaway to celebrate. They both felt relaxed, knowing their next move would involve the right combination of timing and luck.

"Something golden will come along," Karen said. "I can

just feel it. As Gran would say, 'What is yours will never pass you by.'" This was a wonderful period for Tom and Karen had so much to share.

Keywords/Phrases: Well compensated, generous bonus offered, gratitude, acts of kindness, more money than expected, renewed faith, good fortune, give and receive, accept generosity, change and growth.

Further Interpretations: Unexpected windfall, given a gift, pennies from heaven, giving or receiving help, surprises.

Visual Representation: Tom and Karen are extremely grateful that their business finally sold—and for a profitable figure too. Their debts are completely paid off, which brings much happiness. Their generosity flows with acts of charity in appreciation for their staff. In addition to the act of giving, Tom and Karen are on the receiving end of others' generosity and kindness. As you can see, with the Six of Pentacles, money is not stagnant; it is continually moving. You could be on the receiving end of a gift or you could be in the position to give generously. In any case, there is a sense of peace and happiness related this card because it indicates the end of the tribulations expressed with the Five of Pentacles. Money is once again available, and lessons have been learned about its exchange.

Seven of Pentacles

With their resources renewed, Tom and Karen took the time to *look over everything* they had achieved. Their small break away had been good for them both. It gave them time to *reflect on their past efforts* and *ponder their future strategies.* They were pleased with their efforts and in awe of the many life lessons they experienced along their journey. Both were immensely proud of the other. Tom and Karen's relationship had never been as strong as it was then. They had a beautiful new home, two great kids, a wonderful marriage, and enough money available for a comfortable life. What more could they ask for?

Stepping back from the canvas of life, Tom and Karen decided to take a well-deserved rest and enjoy a moment to *stop and review* just how far they had come. One afternoon, drinking a piña colada, lazing by the hotel pool, Karen leaned over and whispered to Tom, "Life doesn't get much better than this."

Tom smiled, happy to see Karen enjoying herself. At dinner that night they laughed at all the mistakes they made at the beginning of their careers and what a huge learning curve owning the store was. They were so happy with what they achieved.

Once home, Tom became restless. He was *eager to start a new project,* so he *pondered his options.* Tom thought about whether it was wise to continue in business or put his energy into something completely new. Late one Sunday, Karen found Tom sitting on the back porch daydreaming about distant places and new adventures. She sat down with him for a while, both enjoying the silence.

"I think it's time for a change," Tom said out of the blue, looking into the distance. "Time to take on new risks."

Karen was not surprised; she knew she couldn't keep an ambitious man like Tom down for too long. She advised him to have patience and *carefully think* his plans through *before acting*. But, Tom, ever the bull in a china shop, decided then and there that the next day he would start making inquiries about selling spare parts online. Unsurprisingly, he had learned a lot over the years in the auto parts business, and he knew exactly what actions were useful for a business like this and which were a waste of his time and effort.

Now, he understood that by starting a new business, he would have to experience the same lessons all over again, just in a different time and place. This time around, though, things were a little different. Tom was now relieved of the pressure he felt when he first opened his store. He was more financially secure now, and his *life was more balanced and stable.* He knew he still had a lot to learn and that he should be extremely careful with his existing finances. He also knew that Karen was right, and at last, he was willing to take her advice: slow down and think this through. Tom knew his decision would have consequences for them both. Fortunately, Tom only placed a one-year non-compete clause in his contract of sale with the store, and that time was fast approaching.

That night, as they got ready for bed, Tom asked Karen, "Where do you want to be in five or ten years' time?"

"I'd be happy if life could stand still and stay exactly as it is right now . . . but I know that's not going to happen." She advised Tom to maybe use only the interest they had on their investments to start his new business and leave the capital in the bank for now and see where the new adventure led.

"You know I am right behind whatever you decide to do," Karen said. Tom showed he was a much wiser man today, and Karen had complete faith in him. She knew he would think it through well before acting on it.

Keywords/Phrases: Look over everything, reflect on past efforts, ponder your future strategies, step back from the canvas of life, stop and renew, restless, ponder your options, think carefully before acting, balance life, think this through

Further Interpretations: A temporary pause, reflection, contemplation, temptation, a need to weigh-up an offer, assess what needs to be done, self-evaluation, move through the change.

Visual Representation: The Seven of Pentacles offers some time for Tom to look back and review just how far he has come. All his achievements lay before him, but he is restless and yearns for more. Tom must now contemplate the value of his efforts, what experiences were gained, and the rewards of his hard work. However, there is a decision looming in the air, and this choice is at the root of his contemplation. Re-evaluation and redirection are clearly on his mind. The next chapter of success awaits.

Eight of Pentacles

Over the next few weeks, Karen hardly saw Tom. He may have surfaced from a book for a quick bite at lunch time, but he'd quickly disappear back into his office and not surface again until dark. He had his *head down and bum up, learning* all there was to know about online marketing. He had enrolled in an online computer course and told Karen he was loving it. This surprised Karen, as Tom had never really shown an interest in office work before now, typically preferring to leave all the books to her. He told Karen that it was like being *back at school,* that there was *so much to learn.*

Occasionally, Tom would ask Karen for her advice if he felt stuck on something, but generally he was a very *fast learner.* Just the other day, Tom had a problem saving his work to a smart drive, but Karen sorted it all out and got him back on track. Alice made a comment to her mother one day about the number of hours her dad was spending in his office.

"Your father has a huge *thirst for knowledge* at the moment," Karen told the kids. "He is enjoying the process of *learning new skills* and is putting in a *huge effort* for his *new project.*"

Tom was feeling great enthusiasm and interest in this new form of selling. He was full of *fresh energy* because he once again had a goal he 100 percent knew he would achieve. Tom took great *pride in his work* and was motivated to make his new business a success. He worked diligently day after day, buying, cataloguing, and listing his new stock. Tom's past experiences with the store had given him *invaluable knowledge* on what to purchase. He knew exactly the quality of products needed. But purchasing stock was just a small part of his new venture. Tom still had *a lot to learn* and master.

Tom had once again found his spark, his passion, his purpose. This job was a labour of love. Karen was pleased to see Tom so happy and his spirit full of ignited dedication. Tom told Karen that his new business had not only sparked his enthusiasm about *acquiring new skills,* but it was also a relief that he had not exhausted all his potential and there was still life within him to manifest anything he desired.

One day, Peter and Dot asked Karen while she was visiting if she thought Tom was suffering from a midlife crisis. Karen simply laughed.

"No not at all," she replied. "Tom knows this is a time to think long term and is engaged in seeing his ideas turn into his greatest riches."

Karen was right. Tom's hard work continued from sun-up to sundown, and his dedication began to yield true results. Tom was determined to see his new business work and *bring his dream to life.* He told Karen, "I must think long-term and pay no attention to the fluctuations in my experience."

Every day he learned more, and every day his skills improved. "Practice makes perfect," Gran would say. *Remain true to yourself, and your authenticity will keep you in alignment with miracles.* His diligence and hard work were their own reward, and his effort spoke for itself. His endurance, strength, and fortitude carried him all the way. Tom was happy to report to Karen that his new business was finally showing a profit.

Keywords/Phrases: Head down, bum up, study, back to school, so much to learn, thirst for knowledge, new skills, huge effort, new project, fresh energy, pride in his work, invaluable knowledge, acquiring a new skill, practice makes perfect, bring dreams to life.

Further Interpretations: Apprentice, perfecting, invest in long-term goals, new area, career or direction, back to the drawing board, mastering your craft, enjoying your employment, a productive day, commitment, refinement, just doing it.

Visual Representation: With the energy of the Eight of Pentacles, Tom undertakes an apprenticeship. This offers Tom time to learn new skills; it's a time to begin something he has not previously done. A new creative venture is underway. In this case, Tom is about to experience a change or new beginning in terms of work, education, and financial circumstances. He is determined to master a new skill. This card is the herald of success through perseverance and initiative. Tom is prepared to invest time and energy into his new direction. He is sure to be successful because he is working in a positive manner to make things happen, resulting in a rewarding and profitable end.

Nine of Pentacles

Through hard work, self-control, discipline, and focus, Tom had reached a *comfortable position financially*. He was *incredibly proud* of his new business, and he had actually hired a virtual assistant to lessen the workload so he could sit back and *enjoy the fruits of his labour*. Isac also had been working with him on weekends, and Tom enjoyed that immensely. He hoped that one day Isac would be interested in taking over his business.

Karen never doubted Tom's ability to *master and conquer* for one minute and was delighted at how successful his business had become. She had been busy decorating their new home and failed to notice just how *happy and content* Tom really was. No matter what she was doing, though, Karen always found time if Tom needed her assistance. Some days she helped him fulfil orders and run errands so he could relax for a little. Tom was thrilled with his *success and independence*. He felt a sense *of profound satisfaction and fulfilment* had been achieved with the realization that he *had built something enduring*. He felt he had finally *left a mark* of some kind, that his life was not just a meaningless flicker that vanished.

Now that things were steadily going well with the new business, it was time for Tom to treat Karen to the finer things in life. They had both worked hard and deserved to treat themselves! They got away for a few days to their favourite bed-and-breakfast to *relish in their success.*

"I feel like I am finally being paid for all the times I wasn't paid. This time away was just what I needed to gain perspective and *appreciate just how far we have come.* A time to look back and see the difference we have made," Tom told Karen over dinner.

Self-confidence paired with *self-discipline* had brought Tom rewards on many levels. He knew he absolutely had to remain grounded for things to flow smoothly for him. His past taught him well. His success was no accident; it was packed full of hard work and commitment. He had *passed a test of time.* Tom had to remind himself to stop and enjoy the blessings that had been bestowed upon him. Even Peter and Dot told Karen how proud they were of him and that they never once doubted his abilities to be successful in whatever he chose to do. Peter also said that Tom was a self-made man who put in the effort on his own, without needing anybody else, and as such, he *deserved all the rewards* that brought. Karen loved her parents and remembered their concerns in the early days when Tom seemingly had a *wild* imagination.

"I never doubted Tom's abilities for one minute," Karen replied.

Tom felt confident in where his life was heading. He had acted from a place of wisdom and had been cautious with his decision-making. Now, it was time to relax and enjoy life. Karen thought it was time for an overseas vacation; she had always wanted to travel. *Life was good,* and both Karen and Tom had earned a few weeks away to replenish their souls.

Lying in bed that night, Tom told Karen how much he loved and appreciated her. "I feel like I have had a life worth living. I know I took on life's challenges regardless of the consequences and feel like I have fulfilled my destiny." Karen snuggled in closer to Tom, feeling so proud of the man she married.

Keywords/Phrases: Comfortable position, incredibly proud, enjoy the fruits of your labour, master and conquer, happy and content, success and independence, profound satisfaction, fulfilling, built something enduring, left a mark, relish in your success, appreciate just how far you have come, self-confidence, self-discipline, passed the test of time, deserves all the rewards, life is good.

Further Interpretations: Achievements, sitting pretty, abundance, good health, dreams fulfilled, time of healing, using all your resources, success on your own merit, financial gain, diligent, disciplined, being successful, deserving.

Visual Representation: Tom has reached a point in his life where he is feeling self-confident, self-sufficient, and self-reliant. He is able to stand tall and feel pride. He has attained well-deserved success and may now enjoy the money, leisure time, pleasure, and material comforts success brings. This rest is well-deserved. He appreciates what is available to him and knows that his financial difficulties are over. The Nine of Pentacles denotes the ability to complete any work necessary with confidence, self-discipline, and patience.

Ten of Pentacles

Tom and Karen's home burst with *abundance.* Their world was a lush, vibrant garden they got to enjoy every day. They had successfully built a foundation that will *provide* for themselves and their children *well* into the future. They had worked hard and entered a *sweet time* of their lives, enjoying the *land of milk and honey—a dream* many could only wish for. It was a time when all their senses were awakened to *the unlimited possibilities* life had to offer. *Family life was flourishing,* and Tom and Karen had so much to be grateful for. It was a precious time, a time when they both acknowledged that all their *needs had been met. Joy and contentment, a real sense of fulfilment.*

"I have this inner warmth that *all is well.* I can feel Gran wrapping us up in her big, soft arms. I feel so at peace," Karen said one night before bed.

"I know exactly how you feel," Tom replied, snuggling closer to Karen. "There is a feeling of liberation that comes from actually being happy, feeling *joy for the sake of joy.* I remember Gran saying, 'Your soul has always known you could accomplish anything if it brought you joy. Joy does not simply happen to us. We have to choose joy and keep choosing it every day.'"

"Everything just seems to *fall into place* for us. I guess we should enjoy each breath and each *glorious moment,*" Karen said as she snuggled even closer.

Tom knew deep within the *importance of family*, and he cherished Karen more than she would ever know. He valued her opinion more than anyone else's. She had been his grounding rock when he needed to be reined in and pulled back down to earth. They made a dynamic combination in business together, which at times tested their closeness. Tom's determination to have a *successful business life* had made him pay a price with his sanity, but that night the past was behind them. *Material security* was what Tom wanted most for his family, and he was so grateful he still had his family to enjoy it with.

There was a *richness to living* floating in their house, and it was all because of how diligently the two of them had devoted their time and energy to get there. Many sacrifices were made, but through it all, Tom and Karen tried to always put Isac and Alice's needs first.

"That's the beauty of being your own boss," Karen always said. "I can always be there when the children are sick or attend their many school functions." Tom, on the other hand, felt he may have missed too much of their children growing up, but he was home every night and always took the time to be there for them both.

Nonetheless, it was a time in their life when they sought their true north. Great love and support surrounded them. Both Tom and Karen knew what really mattered in life was a strong family, held tightly *together with love*. That was the *happily-ever-after* feeling.

Keywords/Phrases: Abundance, provide well, sweet time, land of milk and honey, a dream, unlimited possibilities, family life flourishing, all is well, joy for the sake of joy, glorious moments, importance of family, successful business life, material security, richness in living, strong family held together with love, happy ever after.

Further Interpretations: End and beginning, inheritance, spending money on the home, retirement, leaving a legacy.

Visual Representation: Ten is the number of completion and the subsequent new beginnings. It's like a springboard. With the Ten of Pentacles, wealth has been secured. The Pentacles are solid, earthy, heavy, not emotional, inspirational, or mental. They are the essence of the earth and manifestation in the "real" world. This card is about reaching a comfortable space where our goals have been achieved, rewards have been dealt, and we have time to breathe before we start our next adventure. Family is everything to Tom and Karen, and they have finally reached financial security; everything has fallen into line, and at last, they've accomplished their goals of a well-established career. Both of them are proud to be successful and are good at what they do to provide their family with the financial security needed to build a good lifestyle. Tom can rest easy and live happily ever after.

PAGE of PENTACLES.

Page of Pentacles

Over a quiet beer late one afternoon, all of Tom's idle thoughts were focused on what could be in store for his and Karen's future. His idea of running an online business was only in *the early stages* of development, and he had been *offered some good advice* from a trusted friend in the online marketing industry. He had *enrolled in a few courses* that would teach him everything he needed to know to get started. Tom was brimming with excitement to see his *creative pursuit* materialize. He was *up for the task* of extended learning and was eager to fully *pursue a new challenge.*

Karen was happy for Tom, as she had noticed that he had become restless, searching for further tasks to fulfil. Once again Tom had found his direction and calling.

Tom's plans budded in his imagination, and he knew there was much *work ahead* before any results could be realised. His plans needed to be *nurtured* before they could develop into something tangible. This time around, he had experience behind him. He brought all his resources together and used his foresight to stay on track, remembering Gran's famous words, "If you fail to plan, you plan to fail." Planning was the first step Tom had to take before he could be successful. He had placed a small amount of money aside for projects like this and needed to spend it wisely. Karen and Tom were both aware that care, gentleness, and time were needed to bring their potential reward to fruition.

Tom had been *offered many opportunities.* His friends knew how much of *a reliable, clever, hardworking, kind, and dependable* man Tom was and would love for him to work for them. But Tom had been his own boss for too long, and he was eager to start something of his own. This time, he prepared the *fertile grounds* of his business so each aspect of it could withstand pressure later on when things began rolling. Tom was ready to live up to everyone's high expectations. He definitely had more *patience and determination* to see his new creative venture succeed.

Keywords/Phrases: Early stages, offered good advice, creative pursuit, up for the task, new challenges, workload ahead, nurtured, offered many opportunities, reliable, clever, hardworking, kind, dependable, fertile ground, patience, determination.

Further Interpretations: Plants many seeds of growth, new business, new skills, begin a new journey toward healing, full of faith, clear energy, birth of new form, manifestation, a plan.

Visual Representation: The Page of Pentacles, like the pages of all the suits, is a card of new beginnings, inspiration, and the initial stages of a creative project or venture. Tom is absorbed by the coin in his hands, which represents his goals and dreams and the desire to fulfil those dreams in the material world. This card represents the beginning of a new educational experience. It does not indicate the fulfilment of dreams as much as the initial motivation and energy to begin the process of making those dreams a reality. Castles in the sky may be beautiful in theory, but now is the time to begin to put foundations under them. Tom has the desire to learn all things. He is dedicated to attaining wisdom. He is once again totally enthused by the prospects of his new business venture. His inexperience does not faze him at all.

Knight of Pentacles

KNIGHT of PENTACLES.

Tom had a lot to *think over*, and late one afternoon Karen found him in his favourite chair in the garden, lost in thought. He sat *patiently, contemplating his best options.* He had a *good business head* and was *not rash* with his decisions; he preferred *pondering his motives* this time around. He was not ruled by any emotions, which Karen found pleasing to see. Nonetheless, Tom had his *plan under control.* He was a *kind man* with a loyal heart, and Karen knew it was best to give him space when he was thinking, as Tom rarely left anything undone. He was *methodical* in nature, even *venturesome at times.* Karen knew that Tom would see to every detail and take his time.

Tom had *realistic expectations* about how far he could go with his new ideas. Forever the *seeker of knowledge,* Tom had become completely comfortable in his skin and with the ordinary tasks of living. For once, he refrained from jumping too far ahead, and he now understood the importance of *hard work,* responsibility, and *continued perseverance.* Karen admired Tom for taking the time to sit and think; she expressed later that night how proud she was of him. He told her that he had been thinking a lot of his Nana Flo and knew that she was with him.

"She would say, '*In stillness, you receive,*' and '*Silence is never empty, it is full of answers.*' Now I finally get it."

At last, Tom felt he had everything under control. He was taking his time to know exactly what the investments of his time, energy, and money would bring him. Karen suggested that he try working for others for a change of pace, but Tom preferred to have his own business; he *detested being told what to do* by others. He sought control over his life by working, learning, and organising his future. Tom was *a visionary.* He knew what he wanted and internally vowed to let *nothing stand in his way.* If he wanted something done, he never waited around for others to do it for him. He always preferred to do it himself, whatever it took, something his pops taught him when he was a child.

Keywords/Phrases: Patient, contemplation, best options, good business mind, not rash, ponders his motives, plans under control, kind, methodical, venturesome, realistic expectations, seeker of knowledge, hard worker, continued perseverance, taking his time, detest being told what to do, visionary, nothing stands in his way.

Further Interpretations: Wise investments, sit and think awhile, lacks physical energy, trustworthy, devoted, business wins over emotions, mastery.

Visual Representation: The Knight of Pentacles comes in slow and steady upon his steed. This time round, Tom takes his time to cross all his T's and dot all his I's. He is conventional, methodical, and leaves nothing to chance. He accepts responsibility easily. Tom is very trustworthy and steadfast and is a person with the patience to accomplish all his tasks. He is reliable due to his sense of responsibility. He and Karen now enjoy the simple things in life and everything it has to offer. Their efforts will be rewarded in more ways than one. Tom is active in a boring but persistent way. He is loyal and patient and will diligently finish what he starts. He is very much concerned with fulfilling obligations. He is an impassive, indifferent, and stoic man who does not always take the feelings of others into account. He is very traditional, clever with his money, patient, and hardworking.

Queen of Pentacles

Tom and Karen were both wonderful people. They both had big hearts and loved to *nurture* each other. They tried as often as they could to have quality time together and *care tremendously* for their friends and family. Friends could always count on Karen for her *practical, wise advice.* Her *warm, happy, calming, earthy* personality easily attracted friends. Tom said she could be stubborn at times, but he loved her more than ever. "Karen is my rock."

Tom understood the need for Karen's business input and was willing to compromise for them both to progress. Together, they made an unstoppable team. At times, they expected and demanded a great deal from each other. Karen, in particular, had *a way with people.* Her *feminine strength* and sensuality could tame the hardest of men. If ever a customer was upset with a product or complained at the store, Karen would step out of her office and, within a few seconds, have everything under control. Ever *pragmatic and protective of her wealth* and territory, Karen was a force unto herself. She *was independent, strong, self-sufficient, and hardworking.* She was also *generous* and willing to indulge herself and others when it suited her. Tom, at times, worried about finances but trusted that Karen knew how to secure money and energy.

Tom and Karen loved to give generously to those in need. Karen worked with many charities, *giving her time freely.* She also took time to *indulge herself* but always remained fit and healthy. She paid attention to her diet and exercised regularly.

Karen always made time to be there for Tom whenever he needed her. Tom could count on Karen to keep the household secure and running smoothly. She possessed an *endurance and stability* that were admired by others. Karen jumped at the chance to work at the store and oversee the finances when Tom first mentioned his ideas to her.

Tom admired Karen's *good business sense* when it came to juggling the figures so there was always money available. Before they were married, Karen worked at a bank and was considering becoming an accountant; that was before Isac was born. Karen never regretted giving up on a career to raise her family. Now that the couple was stable, she devoted her spare time to caring for her wonderful gardens. She had a real green thumb. Tom said Karen could potter about in the yard for hours, but Karen said being a part of nature keeps her feeling whole and grounded.

Keywords/Phrases: Big heart, nurturer, cares tremendously, practical and wise advice, warm, happy, calming, earthy, has a way with people, feminine strengths, pragmatic, protective of her wealth, independent, strong, self-sufficient, hard-working, gives her time freely, indulges herself, endurance and stability, good business sense.

Further Interpretations: Faithful, can be stubborn, insecure at times, compassionate, sensuous, domesticity, fertility, resourceful, grounded, down to earth, honest, cares for her health.

Visual Representation: Karen is the original Earth Mother. She's the one with rows of home-cooked canned goods on the shelf in the root cellar. She is able to work a full-time job, take care of the children, keep the house clean, and still have time to read the financial section of the *Wall Street Journal*. She most likely has a secret nest egg tucked away in a few bank accounts. Her style of mothering is practical, down-to-earth, and relaxed. She is pragmatic, sensuous, generous, abundant, practical, and an astute businesswoman. Karen is capable and practical in business, but she can be happy either in the workforce or at home. She likes enjoying her material comforts.

KING of PENTACLES.

King of Pentacles

Ever humble, Karen was in awe of how easily Tom could put his plans into action. He possessed *strong leadership qualities* that others had no choice but *respect*. Tom's plans always seemed to end in the best outcome. He had always been a *good provider,* and Karen knew she was a lucky girl to have found such a wonderful *hardworking man,* but at times, he could be a little *materialistic.* We all have our faults, don't we?

Tom was the more *practical* one in their relationship. He was very *accomplished* and strove to succeed at whatever he put his mind to. Karen had often said that Tom had the *Midas touch.* Everything he touched turned to gold. He had the ability *to manifest whatever he wanted* because of his dedication and intense focus on his goals. He had the desire for power and *material security* and prided himself on working hard to earn the life he had. He loved a challenge and was not content with comfort. Karen said Tom's spirit was "dynamic."

Tom had reached the top of his field due to his *leadership qualities, ambition, realism,* and *discipline* to overcome whatever obstacles laid in his path. Karen was aware that Tom had learned his lesson on putting his ambition before everything else. He had grown in confidence and had mastered his natural gift of manifestation.

Tom felt optimistic about his new career path; he believed anything was possible. He felt capable of achieving whatever he desired. Karen thought Tom was a bit *overconfident,* warning him about taking on more than he could comfortably handle. Tom knew how to manage his capabilities but nonetheless was careful not to overreach.

When Dot and Peter visited later in the week, Dot asked Karen why Tom could never rest.

"Is it not enough for him to just retire and enjoy life without the added stress of starting a new business?" her mother inquired.

Karen simply replied, "No, it is not."

Keywords/Phrases: Strong leadership qualities, respected, good provider, hard-working, materialistic, practical, accomplished, has the Midas touch, can manifest whatever he wants, material security, ambitious, realistic, disciplined, overconfident.

Further Interpretations: Values what is material, ruthless, career success, resists change, powerful, places money and career before relationships, solid and wise investor, uses common sense, magnetic, stable, reliable, generous, very good businessman.

Visual Representation: Karen loves Tom's responsible nature and trustworthiness. He is slow to anger and cares deeply for his family. He is a good provider and an excellent husband and father, so long as his authority is not disputed. While he is an extremely hard worker, conscientious, and reliable, Karen notices that Tom can be a little closed-minded at times. He only believes in what he can see, touch, hear, taste, or smell; anything else is highly suspect. If not for Grans teachings, Tom could become quite a sceptic.

THE CUPS

THE CUPS

"Love and compassion are necessities not luxuries;
without them humanity cannot survive."
—Dali Lama

The Cups in the Tarot deck are likened to the Hearts in a regular playing deck. Cups represent water, the west, and autumn. They represent love, emotions, decisions, sensitivities, and family life. Since the Cups focus most on the emotional level of consciousness, they mirror our spontaneous responses and habitual reactions to situations. Cups are associated with anything emotional, from marriage to personal possessions and concerns. They also cover anything relating to partnerships, whether in a work or personal context. All in all, this suit is one of love and happiness, and the feelings suggested by it run deep.

Ace of Cups

After such a turbulent year selling the store and building their new house, Karen thought it would be nice to spend some quality time away with Alice. "Just the girls," she told Tom. Tom thought it was a great idea and knew how much it would mean to Karen. He assured her that he would be fine with Isac for a week or two. Karen stopped by the travel agency the next day on her way home from the shops. After being shown all the wonderful places to stay, Karen decided to book a lovely room for seven nights in a five-star beach resort in Fiji.

Karen and Alice had a special kind of closeness. Their friends often commented that it was easy to tell they were mother and daughter. Alice had the same long, blonde, flowing hair and piercing emerald green eyes as her mother. They were very similar in nature too, even though Karen thought Alice was a lot more mature at fifteen than she ever was. Both Isac and Alice were wonderful young adults. Isac was much like his father in looks, "a very handsome young man," Karen would say. He was tall and athletic, much like Tom was at his age, but Isac had Karen's eyes and blonde sandy hair, unlike Tom's dark features. Isac quite often had young girls calling the house to see him. Alice said most of her girlfriends drooled over him. "They only want to be my friend so I will introduce them to my brother," she'd say with an eye roll. Isac was his own man, though, much like his father, and was not interested in girls at that stage of his life. He was more into cars and hanging with his mates.

Alice was over the moon when her mother told her of their vacation plans. They were leaving the following Saturday, but Karen noticed that Alice had her bags packed on Monday; she was so keen to get away. This would be Alice's first trip overseas.

The flight over was enjoyable, and they arrived safely just after lunch, Fiji time. After they checked in to their hotel and settled into their room, they spent the afternoon relaxing by the pool and recovering from their early morning and long flight. The weather was glorious, with not a cloud in the sky. It was hot but not too hot. Still, Karen made sure they both wore sunscreen and a hat, considering they both had fair skin that burned easily. Karen didn't want sunstroke to spoil their holiday.

On their first night, they decided to eat at the resort restaurant for dinner. They had a wonderful meal of fresh seafood, and when they finished, they decided to take a walk along the beach. Strolling along the water's edge, Alice asked her mother how she met her dad.

"Was it *love* at first sight?" she said with a giggle.

Karen and Alice sat down in the sand, and Karen began.

"I was about your age when I met your father. He was a friend of my brother, your Uncle Peter. They both played on the same football team. I would occasionally go to watch Peter play. It wasn't my thing, but your nan would insist I go and often dragged me along with her.

"I remember this day well. It was freezing cold and raining cats and dogs. I actually thought it was going to snow. I *really* didn't want to be there. I stayed for the first half, bored senseless. You could hardly see the players sloshing in the mud. I had no idea which one was Peter. So, your nan gave me permission to meet some of my friends at the mall. The rain was bucketing down, so I waited under the grandstand steps for it to ease up.

"That was when your dad appeared from *out of nowhere* and offered me an umbrella. He told me he played with my brother Peter but had recently broken his leg and was watching the game from the stands behind us. I never really noticed your dad before that day, but zing went the strings of my heart! I was *smitten*. I accepted the umbrella and thanked him before clumsily making a run for it to meet my friends. Later that day, when I got home, I remember drilling Peter with a hundred questions about Tom.

"I had never really felt those *feelings* before. I tried to talk with your nan while she was cooking dinner, but she just smiled and said Tom was too old for me and I was too young to be thinking of boys. But from that day, I never missed a football match. I spent many nights trying to define the feelings that had made their way into my life. I knew your nan and pop were not going to allow me to date, so I tried to put my feelings to the side and wait. My friends were sick of hearing about Tom anyway."

Keywords/Phrases: Love, falling in love, zing went my heart strings, smitten, new feelings, love appears from nowhere.

Further Interpretations: New relationships, beginnings, positive new emotions, romantic, birth, new feelings of love for someone or something, affection, trust your intuition to lead you to happiness, balance, flow.

Visual Representation: The Ace of Cups represents the first stirring of feelings within Karen's heart. The act of falling in love is blissful and will open the person up to supreme happiness. In Karen's recollection of her first encounter with Tom, her cup overflows with joy and love. This signals an emotional upsurge of new emotions. This cup symbolises emotional fulfilment, not just on an emotional level, but on the spiritual level as well. There's an abundance of love, joy, and celebration associated with this card.

Two of Cups

Karen continued, "My infatuation faded over time, so I put your dad out of my mind and got on with my life. About three years later, while standing in the checkout line at the grocery store, I dropped my bag. I bent down to pick it up and bumped heads with someone. When I stood back up, rubbing my head, I was shocked to see it was your dad. He was standing in line behind me. We locked eyes, and my heart jumped. I remembered him from the day at the football field all those years ago and nervously said hello. Something sparked between your dad and me; we both felt a *strong connection,* like we were being *pulled together* by outside forces beyond our control.

"We both recognised each other from the day at the football field, and he said, 'Hi, you're Peter's sister, Karen.' I shyly said yes. We made small talk about the weather, both feeling a little nervous. He apologised to me for hitting heads and offered to carry my bags to the car. We walked out into the carpark in silence, both not knowing what to say. I was very shy back then, and my stomach was doing cartwheels. I don't think I could have spoken even if I had something interesting to say. Tom handed me my bags and said goodbye.

"When I got home from the store, I wondered if your dad felt the same way I did. He was quiet and guarded regarding his *attraction* to me. Was I being foolish to think he liked me too? Later that day, he called and asked me out to dinner. I tried not to sound too excited over the phone, so I said yes as calmly as I could. I remember squealing with joy after hanging up the phone. I was ecstatic. I raced to my room and must have tried on every outfit I owned. I wanted to look right, sexy but not provocative.

"I rang my best friend Megan to tell her the news. She was just as excited as I was. We decided the best course of action was to remain very low-key and not read too much into our first date. You know, pretend not to show too much interest, play hard to get. Your dad later said that was what he most liked about me and *attracted* him to me in the first place: the fact that I didn't chase him.

"After the night of our first date, we were *inseparable* and so *in love*. Our *relationship* was so strong, and I'm sure it could have moved mountains. We just clicked, and being with your dad *felt* so *right*. It felt as if I had known your dad my whole life. We *connected* on everything. We both loved the outdoors and liked the same music. We even liked the same food. I knew right there and then, on our first date, that he was the man for me. I had a *deep inner knowing* that he was the one.

"Your dad once told me he was sure his Nana Flo had something to do with us *coming together*. I never meet your dad's gran, but I am sure you have heard him talk of her a fair bit over the years. He really loved her and misses her immensely. Gran was a huge part of your dad's life when he was growing up. When she passed, he said a part of him died with her. Your dad and I both knew we would be *together* and that our relationship would *create something amazing*, something we could never have achieved on our own or with another. All my friends loved Tom too. Those were such *happy days*. I hope you meet a man as good as your dad someday."

Keywords/Phrases: Strong connection, attraction, inseparable, in love, feels right, connected, deep inner knowing, create something special, amazing, happy days.

Further Interpretations: Union, kindred spirits, romance blooms, magnetic connection, making a commitment, partnership, co-create, affinity.

Visual Representation: The feelings and outpouring of love felt with the Ace of Cups have now found a home. With the Two of Cups, beauty and power are created when two hearts become one. Relationships are cemented, and commitments are established. A new friendship, romance, or partnership is going to begin, with a chance for love and affection. This card shows that Tom and Karen have an emotional affinity, sympathy, and harmony together. They both feel a mutual bond with each other.

Three of Cups

"What was dad like back then?" Alice asked. "He seems so intense now; I can't imagine him being the *fun*, life of the *party* type."

"Your dad has changed a little over the years," Karen said. "But the fun-loving Tom is still inside. He has a strong work ethic that was instilled in him when he was young, not from his dad but from his pops. Your dad finds it hard to relax and enjoy time away from work. Work is his passion."

"So how did Dad propose?" Alice asked, feeling excited to hear the whole story.

"Your dad and I had been dating for almost a year. I was thinking that *life didn't get any better.* Love has a way of making rust look like gold. At that time, your dad was working as a mechanic, and I was working at the bank, so we never had much time to see each other during the week. Every weekend, though, we shared our life with *good friends, partying* and having a really *great time.* We had a fantastic group of like-minded friends, and Tom and I were so in love.

"Just before midnight as the party was really starting to get wild, your dad got down on one knee, pulled out a ring, and asked me to *marry* him. All I could say was 'Wow' because I was shocked. I never saw that coming. I remember crying as your dad put the ring on my finger. I had never felt that kind of happiness before. Everyone went crazy, hugging us and shaking Tom's hand. I remember afterward, with all the excitement, we both got extremely drunk, which you know is something I rarely do. That was the best night of my life, one I will never forget. We *drank and danced* well into the morning. When I woke up the next day, I checked my finger because I thought it was all a dream. But the ring was there. I loved it, and it fitted perfectly," Karen said while fiddling with the ring. "This will be yours one day.

"Your nan and pop were thrilled when I showed them my ring. Unbeknownst to me, your dad had already been around to the house and asked your pop for his permission to marry me. That little sneak! Nan joked that he had asked weeks ago, and she wondered when he would get around to it. I told her he was quite drunk when he asked, so I guess he needed to build up his confidence.

"We were married about three months later, and what a *celebration* that was! We had over one hundred guests at our *wedding*. Your Aunt Terese was my maid of honour, and Uncle Peter was your dad's best man. My friend Megan was my bridesmaid. We preferred to have a small bridal party, but I can assure you it was a huge day. Your dad was so nervous, he dropped the ring twice in the church. Peter had to scramble under the pews to find it. Everyone thought that was hilarious.

"There is not a day that goes by that I don't give thanks and gratitude for all I have. You and your brother have made our family whole. Your dad can sometimes be a bit of a work-aholic, but he has always put me and you kids first. I am so happy I married him, but I don't think I had a choice. The universe wanted us *together* right from the first meeting at the football field all those years ago. We were *destined* to find each other that I know for certain." Alice hugged her mother tightly.

Keywords/Phrases: Fun, party, life doesn't get any better, good friends, great times, marriage, celebrations, destined to be together.

Further Interpretations: Like-minded, social, collaboration, enjoying the company of friends, public recognition, improved health, joining social groups, circle of support, kick up your heels, family, companionship, abundance, sharing, community, happiness.

Visual Representation: The Three of Cups represents the arrival of happy times and all types of celebrations, parties, weddings, and get-togethers. Life is good. On this card, three young maidens dance in a circle with their golden goblets raised in a toast of joy. The ground is covered with fruit, and there is a general sense of abundance and happiness. The Three of Cups indicates the end or conclusion of any past problems. A compromise will be found that will serve the interests of those involved in the potential struggle. Happy times are contagious. The number three typically suggests the initial completion of a project or venture, and in this case, it points to Tom and Karen's wedding, the birth of a child, or the successful initial fulfilment of a goal. However, despite the satisfaction offered by the number three, this card also suggests a new beginning; the celebration is only the start of a long and possibly difficult journey.

Four of Cups

"It hasn't always been roses with your dad and me," Karen continued. "We have had our ups and downs over the years."

Alice was not surprised to hear this, as she often chose to stay out with friends when her parents were going through a hard time, like when they sold the store.

"I know," Alice said.

"We had only been married a few months when your dad was offered a new mechanics position about one hour away from our hometown. He would stay at a friend's house during the week and come home on weekends. I was *not* at all *happy* with that arrangement. I became *disappointed* in Tom, *disillusioned* about our marriage, and despondent about everything. I became *bored* with my life and felt like I couldn't go out with my friends without him. I missed him immensely. Your dad tried to explain to me that this new job paid well, and we needed the money to buy our own home. That was the only way we could get ahead. I knew he was right, but still, I kicked up a fuss.

"I was still very young, naïve, and disillusioned about what marriage really was. I was selfish too; I only thought of my feelings, not your dad's. I built a wall around me and shut him out. I refused to understand why he had to work so far away when there were good jobs closer to home. My friends didn't help either. They were totally on my side and crucified Tom for his actions. But your poor dad was only doing what he knew was the right thing if we were to have a future. I tried not to listen to my friends, but my loneliness overruled me.

"For a long time, I was very *discontent;* not even my friends could cheer me up. I was blind to any form of compromise. I focused too much attention on what I didn't have in my life without appreciating everything I did have. I wanted your dad closer. I would often go off *alone and sulk,* but that was so unlike me. I didn't like the person I was becoming and neither did your dad. My *blindness and ignorance* tested our marriage.

"I had these strange feelings of being let down and cheated by your dad, but really, I was the one who was cheating because of my *unreal expectations.* My life was lacking in magic and excitement. I felt these feelings were only achievable with your dad by my side. On the weekends, when your dad would come home, we did nothing but argue. I wouldn't listen. I was too *narrow* in my *focus* and blocked out his reasoning. Your nan said to me one day, 'Stop acting like a spoilt brat. It's time to grow up.'

"She was right of course. One day, Kristine, a friend I had not seen since our wedding day, stopped by the bank. We chatted for a while, and she told me she could tell something was not OK. I told her about Tom working away from home and how much I missed him. She invited me to join her group that met every week. It was a spiritual group that taught medi-tation. She thought it would be good for me. I went along and had a great night. Over the following weeks of my meditation practice, I began to feel more fulfilled and whole. In the group, I learned that the more centred you are on the inside, the less you need from the outside. The meetings were a little unsettling at first, but the more I absorbed what they were teaching me, the more I was able to relax and open up to happiness from the inside. I told your dad all about this group when he returned. He was thrilled and said it was something he was sure Gran would agree with. He told me that, as a child, he and his brother would meditate with Gran on the farm. That was a surprise to me; I didn't realize just how open-minded your dad was.

"Sometimes, Alice, we can be *our own worst enemy*. We become so blinded by our *stagnation* and *limiting beliefs* that we cannot see the beauty in life around us and end up sabotaging our well-being. You must look through open eyes to all the possibilities life presents to you. Self-reflection will open you up to a happier life. Remind me tomorrow to teach you meditation. It's something I should have taught you years ago. Meditating is what changed me. The more I focused on going within, the stronger I became. I began to be reacquainted with myself and find balance and peace even though I was not happy being apart from your dad."

Keywords/Phrases: Not happy, disappointed, disillusioned, despondent, discontent, let down, unreal expectations, alone and sulking, blindness, ignorance, narrow focus, own worst enemy, stagnation.

Further Interpretations: Open your eyes, other possibilities, not seeing the gift, frustration, gossip, dissatisfaction, grass looks greener on the other side, apathy, unfulfilled, not up to your standards, bored, what else is there, internally unsatisfied.

Visual Representation: At times, we have a tendency to look for something outside of ourselves for happiness without appreciating what we already have in front of us. We believe the grass looks greener on the other side and feel generally unfulfilled with our lot in life. With this card, Karen experiences a time of uncertainty and turns inward to find the truth. She had become tired of the same old struggle that had been carrying on for so long. She needed to re-evaluate her life and environment because she knew familiarity bred contempt as well as dissatisfaction and boredom. Nothing offered her satisfaction. There is a need to search for a more stimulating way of life. Karen is apathetic and dwells too much on the things she does not want rather than on what she does want.

Five of Cups

"Over the following months, I still made your dad *miserable* with my whining and complaining. One day he said he wouldn't be coming back, and in that moment, all my plans shattered. Everything I had wished for was gone. My future was all tied up with your dad. I was heartbroken and felt so *isolated and alone.* I remember locking myself in my room and crying for what felt like days. I shut myself off from life, feeling *rejected,* and grieved. If I lost your dad, I lost everything.

"Your nan came over when she heard the news and told me a few truths. She made me a cup of coffee, and we sat at the table. She said I looked a mess, which I did. I hadn't brushed my hair in days, and my eyes were red and swollen from all the tears I had shed. She told me to stop *crying over spilt milk* and go out and clean it up. Stop *blaming* Tom and look at the role you played in this mess. Patch things up with Tom. She said things don't always go to plan, but *all was not lost.* I still had a *chance to change* and *make things right* with him.

"That day I remember she really gave me a dressing down, something I needed to hear. She said that he still loved me and if I could change the way I felt about him working away from home, life would be better. She reminded me that he was only doing it for the money and that he wanted to provide for me. 'He loves you; everyone can see that. Open your eyes!' she said. I could finally see my disgraceful selfish behaviour for what it was and truly *regretted my past actions.* I felt ashamed.

"Your nan was right. I accepted why your dad felt he needed to stay away and hoped we still had a chance to make things right. I recognized what I had with your father, and I wanted him back, even if it was only part-time. My friends in my meditation group were very supportive. They noticed I was not my usually bright happy self, so I explained to them what was happening in my life. I poured out my heart, and they listened. I explained how I had been behaving toward our situation and how *sad* I felt about your dad leaving.

"During one meeting, Kristine asked, 'Do you still love him?' I said, 'Yes, of course.' 'Do you think he still loves you?'

she asked. I said, 'Yes, I am sure of it.' Then, she told me the exact same thing your nan did. I still had a chance of happiness with your dad if I *changed*. It was up to me to take up the challenge and set things right. I forgave myself for my behaviour and asked your dad to do the same. There was no room for regrets. I was determined to make things right again, and through meditation and soul searching, I found true happiness within myself and was able to let go of my clinginess to your dad. If I could give you one piece of advice, Alice, that is to find self-love. Love is an inside job, and the door to your heart can only be opened from the inside. You must love yourself before you can truly love another. Know deep within that you are good enough and loveable and deserve the very best. It was only my *insecurities* that caused the whole *separation* in the first place."

Keywords/Phrases: Miserable, isolated, alone, rejected, crying over spilt milk, blame, all is not lost, chance to change, make things right, regret past actions, sad, insecurities, separation.

Further Interpretations: Disappointed in self, change in focus, change your thoughts, focusing on loss, release regrets, feeling abandoned and unloved, a time to forgive, forget, and move on, resentment, emotional disappointment, sadness.

Visual Representation: In this stage of life, Karen has focused all her energy on her loss, which will not help the situation at hand. To experience the happiness she seeks, she'll need to change her thoughts from worries and regrets and, instead, focus on what she wants: to be reunited with her husband. All is not lost, and Karen must look to the future for the things that are always waiting in the wings. Unfortunately, at the moment, she is disillusioned with life, crying over spilled milk, and feeling generally pessimistic about the future. This is a time for Karen to let go of the past. She has grown considerably from her past mistakes, and now understands that emotional disappointment, depression, and anger are all wasted emotions. Deep regrets are held within the spilled cups, but love is still there in the two that are standing. She must get over her hurt, pick up the remaining cups, and carry on. It is time for Karen to re-evaluate her priorities.

Six of Cups

The next day, while Alice enjoyed some time by the pool with friends she made earlier that morning, Karen decided to go for a nice long walk on the beach. Up to this point, Karen had enjoyed her time away with Alice, but it was nice to have some time on her own to sit in the warm sun and *reminisce*. It was a beautiful sunny day, and the warm sun soothed her soul. Karen sat on the sand, with the wavelets rolling over her feet. She felt so alive yet so at peace.

Her mind *drifted back* to the day she met Tom and to their *many childish pleasures* and *innocent dreams* they shared. A smile crossed her lips as she reminisced about all the good times they shared together in their young lives. The breakup, though painful, helped Karen gain something very precious. She was able to see just how lucky she was and how deeply she loved Tom. Karen knew her love for Tom was deep, and she knew without a doubt that her life would not be as complete as it was now without him in it. Karen sat with her eyes closed, soaking up the sun's rays, her mind *lost in the past.*

She had come to realize that rearing a family and running a business could add a fair amount of stress to any relationship. At times, she felt her and Tom's relationship suffered from a lack of spontaneity. *Habits and patterns* were hard to break, and for a while there, she and Tom had lost a little of their spark. But Karen learned that love heals everything, and with love as a base, you'll always have something worthwhile to build upon. Karen tried not to *romanticise her past* but see it clearly for what it was

After almost an hour passed, Karen sat up in a daze from her *memories.* Feeling that her legs were a little numb, she got up and casually strolled back to the hotel. Karen felt content with her past and where her life was heading. She had a lot of wisdom to pass on to Alice and Isac. She felt safe and secure, and it was a wonderful feeling. She loved that her life was more grounded and full of *familiar patterns.* She was happy and content, and the people around her, even strangers, told her there was a lovely energy surrounding her. She had faced sorrow and pain and knew she never wanted to go there again.

Karen and Alice's time away together had been wonderful but sadly the time had come to head home. Before they boarded their flight home, Alice surprised Karen with a tiny Buddha statue she'd purchased at the local markets. She placed it in Karen's hand and gave her a warm hug.

"I love you, Mum," she said. "This is to remind you of this week away." Karen tried hard to hold back her tears as she hugged her daughter tight. She was so overwhelmed with love for her.

That night, after unpacking, Karen sat outside with Tom and filled him in on the fabulous time she and Alice had together. Karen told Tom how proud she was of the woman Alice was becoming and how she spent some time *reflecting* on her life and how happy she was.

"I had lots of time to just relax and connect back with my true self and replenish my energies," she told Tom. He was pleased that Alice and Karen had a great time away together. He knew all along that they would. Karen and Alice had a very close relationship, one Tom respected and admired.

"You deserve it," he said with a big smile.

Keywords/Phrases: Reminisce, drift back, many childish pleasures, innocent dreams, lost in the past, habits and patterns, romanticise the past, memories, familiar patterns, reflection.

Further Interpretations: Nostalgia, reunions with those from the past, surrendering, past connections, issues involving children, childhood experiences, rekindled relationships, small gesture of kindness, healing, don't get stuck in the past, old flames.

Visual Representation: This card represents a time of lingering regret, nostalgia, and bittersweet memories; however, it also speaks of being hopeful for the future by looking back on your past, even as far back as childhood. The Six of Cups offers us the opportunity to reminisce on the positive, nostalgic memories of joyful times. Spending time with Alice gave Karen a chance to recall her own childhood and many happy memories. Love heals everything.

Seven of Cups

Karen and Alice's time away in Fiji brought them even closer together, not just as mother and daughter but as friends. One day while Karen baked in the kitchen, Alice walked in and asked for advice about something that was troubling her. Karen wiped her hands on her apron and took Alice by the hand. They sat together at the breakfast table, and Karen gave Alice her full attention.

Alice told Karen, "A lot of my friends are leaving school next year and starting their careers, but I'm at a *crossroads* on what to do. I'm confused about *what direction to go* in, and I'm feeling overwhelmed. I have a *lot of options* available, but I'm not sure *which direction to take,*" Alice explained.

Karen told Alice some very valuable advice that she remembered her mother telling her at the same age.

"*Take your time.* Don't rush your decisions," she told Alice. "You are still so young. Spend some quiet time alone with your thoughts to connect with what resonates with you the most. Look closely at all your options and *listen to your intuition.* Your inner voice will provide useful guidance on how to sort through all your options. Some may seem rosy at the moment, but a little further down the line, they may surprise you. *Resist the temptation* to be jealous of your friends. What they do or seek may not be for you. Remember the story I used to tell you as a child about all that glitters? Well, this is one time where what you are looking at may not be all that you expect it to be.

"*Know what you want* from life first," Karen continued. "*Know what you will be happy with,* what you will settle for, and what you can happily live your life doing. Dreams are lovely, and there are so many options out there. You must approach these present opportunities with a definite set of priorities. As your dad's gran would say, if you can dream it, you can have it.

"I have always told you that happiness and contentment come from within. Everything you want will come to you when you know what you want out of life. *Don't* ignore life and *fantasize* about what is not real. Take your time and be clear about what you want and what you can have; accept the limitations of reality. Trust yourself and listen to what your inner self is telling you. The grass is not always greener on the other side of the fence."

Karen gave Alice a reassuring hug and said, "Some of your options may look too good to be true. You will need to *see beyond the superficial.* Some options will be good, some bad. You will know when the time comes. Every option will require hard work and dedication. I trust you will make the right *decision*, but it has to be *your* decision. Only by identifying your needs and wants can you determine how you will meet them. *Listen to your gut;* it will tell you *which road to take.* With this approach, you cannot make a wrong choice. All *choices* lead to lessons you must learn. Your dad would say that his gran was a believer in faith. She would say, 'Whatever belongs to you will never pass you by.'"

Keywords/Phrases: Crossroads, direction, lots of options, take your time, listen to your intuition, resist temptation, know what you want, what you are happy with, don't fantasize, see beyond the superficial, decisions, listen to your gut, which road to take, choices

Further Interpretations: Pause, contemplate, choose wisely, many opportunities, confused, go after what you want, hard work ahead, commitment issues, emotions are scattered, unable to focus, illusions, overindulgence, dreams, manifestations.

Visual Representation: With the Seven of Cups, making emotional decisions is difficult. You must think about your choices and options, but there may be too many opportunities present. You'll need to carefully consider each one to avoid a grave judgment error. On this card, you'll see that there is a cup with a snake and one with a demon. This indicates that though dreaming is beautiful and provides inspiration for action, we must at some point abandon our ideas of "castles in the sky" and begin to build those castles in our real life. A choice must be made even though the apparent abundance of options seems to paralyse us with either fear or excessive anticipation. Karen's advice to Alice is if you are unable to make a decision because of too many options, you may need to carefully evaluate the pros and cons of each option and make a thoughtful choice.

Eight of Cups

After dinner that night, when Tom and Karen were alone, Karen told him about Alice's concerns and the worries she had about her future. They sat in silence for quite a while, lost in their own thoughts.

"Taking the first step is always the hardest," Tom said, breaking the silence. "I mean taking that leap of faith to *start a new journey*. That is where Alice is at the moment. But you were right in telling her that no matter what her choice will be, all experiences will help her grow. Alice is a smart girl; she takes after you. Do not worry too much about Alice; she has a good mind, a beautiful heart, and will know what decision to make.

"I remember when I finally decided to *walk away* and sell the store," Tom continued. "It was something you and I had poured our soul into and really loved. The store was a huge part of us, our life, and our marriage. It was not an easy time, if you can remember. It took a lot of realigning after leaving and selling the store, but bit by bit, I found my feet again. I *found something more fulfilling and rewarding.* I knew deep within that the time had come to sell, even though I put up a fight and clung on to avoid change. I came to the realisation that I had *outgrown* the store, as I lost all pleasure in working there.

"I never told you, but one night, I had a dream, and when I woke the next morning, I just knew I was *meant for something more.* It was a calling *to leave, to go.* It was very strong. All my past experiences have allowed me to face the person I have become. I somehow knew that it was time to sell and everything would be OK."

"It took a lot of *strength and courage to change direction* at our age," Karen said.

"Yeah, it was like, all of a sudden, I no longer wanted to be in the store, and it felt like I just had to drop everything and *walk away.* But I knew I was doing the right thing."

"I always had faith in you, even when you had lost your way," Karen said, taking Tom by the hand. "*Leaving behind* so much of ourselves was painful, but we were not giving up, just *moving forward* for our *emotional growth.* I don't regret it one bit. There is so much *more to life,* and it is not foolish to seek a better existence. This is the moment to acknowledge what we have learned and all the experiences we have gained. The time felt right to *move on* and experience a new way of being. Gran would probably tell you that *your destiny* was calling you."

"I wish Gran was still with us," Tom said. "I know she would tell us that it was *time to walk toward something new.* 'You will no longer benefit or find success by continuing on your path. It is time to *seek out a new life* and let go, as your past journey has come to its conclusion. Endings are always a sign of a new beginning.'

"Alice will make the right choice. She is old enough now to make her own choices and decisions about what she will do. You have reared a sensible young lady. I am very proud of both Isac and Alice. They are both strong and independent and have your kindness. You have done a fabulous job, so don't worry. Alice is your daughter, and she will *follow her heart* when the time comes."

Keywords/Phrases: Start a new journey, walk away, found something more fulfilling and rewarding, meant for something more, leave, go, strength and courage, change direction, leave behind, moving forward, emotional growth, more to life, your destiny, time to walk toward something new, seek out a new life, follow your heart.

Further Interpretations: A spiritual quest, leave the past behind, soul's purpose, leap of faith, there is more waiting for you, withdraw, retreat, moving into the unknown, balancing your spiritual awareness, movement, journey to self-discovery, go it alone.

Visual Representation: Cups contain water, which represents the fluidity of emotions within each of us. There comes a point in everyone's life where, despite how good a situation might seem, it is time to leave. We must move in a direction that is more "air-like," more in touch with reality, and away from emotions. The Eight of Cups symbolises the desire to leave material success behind for something greater. Life is always moving in a new direction, and in the case of Tom and Karen, they desire a new path in life. This is not a time to be afraid to leave the past behind. There's plenty more to see in the world. Don't be disillusioned or lose faith, as the future promises to be brighter. Gran would say, "Follow your heart, do what you desire, and embrace a brand-new you. Your soul is calling."

Nine of Cups

Taking a few moments to relax on the veranda the following day, Karen's mind drifted. She had just stepped out of the hot sun after a hard morning working in the garden. She poured herself a cool drink and sat in her favourite rocking chair. A soft smile crossed her lips as she kicked off her shoes and sighed.

Her mind drifted to how *wonderful her life* was. It didn't get any better than this. Karen felt *completely fulfilled.* Tom had spent the morning working in the garage and noticed Karen sitting quietly on her own. He stopped and watched her for a while. The love he felt for his wife could not get any deeper. Tom sensed just how peaceful Karen seemed. He wandered up to the veranda and sat down next to her, taking her by the hand.

"You look *happy*," he said.

"I am," Karen replied. "I was just thinking about how life feels at the moment. It is so *magical,* and there is *nothing I need* to worry about. My head is clear and at *peace. My heart is full,* and I couldn't be any happier. I feel like all my *dreams have come true;* all my wishes are fulfilled. There is nothing I long for or need. My *cup is overflowing.* If I died today, I would die a happy woman."

"I know how you feel," Tom said. "I feel *satisfied and content,* more so now than at any other time in my life. I think we've finally made it. I think it is time to pat ourselves on the back." Tom kicked off his shoes, and Karen offered him a sip of her cool drink.

"It is such a good feeling," Karen said. "I know you are the one I am meant to be with, my soulmate. I am living where we are meant to be and doing what *fulfils my soul.* What could be better than that? The kids are happy and doing well, the house is my *dream come true,* and I still love you as much as I did when we first met." Tom smiled and quickly picked Karen up, swinging her around.

"Put me down!" she said with a laugh.

As they settled back down, they sat in silence once again, both lost in their thoughts. The *stars had aligned,* and they were so grateful, for fortune had smiled down on them both. *Life was good*, and all was well; worries faded, fears dissolved, and *life was magical. Dreams really did come true.* Karen and Tom were both aware that all their hard work and the hard times were behind them.

"Let's go out and celebrate," Karen suggested. "It has been an emotional journey, and these *feelings* we have are *worth savouring.* This *good energy* we are feeling is something I wish I could bottle and sell. We have much to celebrate, so let's have some fun!"

That settled it and both of them showered and dressed to hit the town.

Keywords/Phrases: Wonderful life, wishes fulfilled, happy, magical, nothing you need, peace, heart is full, dreams come true, cup is overflowing, satisfied, content, fulfils my soul, stars aligned, life is good and magical, spiritual and material success, self-satisfaction, feeling worth savouring, self-satisfaction, great energy.

Further Interpretations: Long-lasting relationships, soulmates, whatever you wish for will come true, family contentment, love and support, happy times, emotional satisfaction, sweet harvest, internal and external happiness, spiritual fulfilment, "I feel good".

Visual Representation: Make a wish, as this card represents a special time in life when everything you've ever wished for can and will come true. Good health and success are assured. At this stage of the journey, Tom and Karen feel fulfilled and stable. The Nine of Cups is a card of great success, especially material success. It represents triumph, victory, and financial well-being. Achievement, satisfaction, wishes fulfilled, self-indulgence, and happiness are certain for the future. Karen and Tom are in awe of their amazing feelings of contentment and physical well-being. They have overcome many difficulties in their past, and now they sit comfortably with emotional stability and a safe outlook. Their inner beings are so secure that they radiate goodwill and happiness in their auras. Dreams really do come true.

Ten of Cups

Tom and Karen went for a delightful stroll together in the park, stopped for lunch at a wonderful new café, and finished off their day with a little shopping. Tom needed some new shirts and aftershave. Karen could not remember the last time she and Tom had had such an enjoyable day together. Over the years, they had spent quite a fair amount of time in each other's company but had always been focused on work, the house, or the children. Today was a day just for them, one Karen hoped to have again soon.

After dinner that night, Alice told Karen how happy she was when she arrived home and found her parents laughing and *having fun together.* Alice helped Karen clean the dishes, then they sat together over a cup of hot chocolate. Tom was in the lounge room watching football, and Isac was at his girlfriend's.

"It is often said that loving another person opens the heart to loving life itself," Karen said to Alice. "Life is bigger and better with more purpose and meaning. Your father and I have a *strong bond of friendship* as well as *love* for each other. We *are committed to each other* and have learned over the years to *give a lot and take a little.* I feel I can be myself with your dad. I am free to pursue whatever fills my desires, knowing your father will always *support* me. Relationships can be a lot of work, but they are so worth it. I hope one day you find the same feelings with someone special.

"Your dad and I have *a beautiful life*. We have immense trust, affection, and love for each other. You know we work hard, but you, your brother, *our family, and our friends are everything* to us. We *have unconditional love to share*; life doesn't get any richer. I have everything I could ever wish or hope for."

Alice hugged her mother tightly. "I hope to be as strong as you, Mum," she said.

Karen looked into Alice's piercing green eyes and said, "Alice, I hope so too, but understand that, in life, there will be cycles. *Joy* and sorrow, *pleasure* and pain, empathy and apathy—that's just the way life goes. It is how you deal with what happens that makes you stronger. Your dad often said his gran would say, 'We can't always choose the music life plays us, but we can choose how we dance to it.'

"Your father and I have had our fair share of challenges that have tested our marriage as well as our purpose, but we are *grateful* for all the lessons that have brought us to this point in our life. We have passed many tests and feel at long last that we have achieved *permanence, meaning, and rightness* in our lives. I cannot explain how *good it feels.*"

Keywords/Phrases: Having fun, strong bonds in friendships and love, commitment to each other, give a lot and take a little, beautiful life, family and friends mean everything, unconditional love to share, joy, pleasure, gratitude, permanence, meaning, rightness, good feelings.

Further Interpretations: Finale, the happy ever after, we finally made it, Hollywood ending, pure joy, complete happiness, family solidarity, you have it all, completion, gather your friends and family, wellbeing, pride, gratitude.

Visual Representation: Life is a fairy tale, and this is the "happily ever after" moment. Happiness, joy, and contentment will dominate your life. The Ten of Cups signifies the satisfying fulfilment of love in a relationship with another. It is a very positive card in terms of relationships and may indicate either the beginning of a new, very happy relationship or the ultimate satisfaction of a long-term relationship. Karen and Tom have all the success they've ever dreamed of. Commitment and love are the requirements of such satisfaction, but this card promises that, with the required effort, lasting love and a happy family life can be built. True friendships and lasting happiness are inspired from above. This is what we call true success. You will never gain more than you have now until you empower yourself by appreciating everything you have done. Everything will work out for the best, and lasting happiness and security is abound with true friendships and a happy family life. This card is the finale to an extraordinary Hollywood event.

PAGE of CUPS.

Page of Cups

Later that night, Karen thought back to the time when she and Tom broke up. She had lost faith in their relationship and her love of life itself. Karen was fragile and delicate, easily hurt and misunderstood, and neither her parents nor her friends could make her see sense.

Karen needed to take some time to find love for herself as an individual. Karen felt she was not whole without Tom. A huge *period of growth* followed their time apart. She was aware that she was on fertile ground with her *new emotions.* She came to the realization that she was now a stronger person within herself. Karen *awakened to her feelings* for Tom as a separate person and not someone who had to prop up her self-sabotaging emotions. Tom and Karen began to communicate better, expressing their feelings openly.

Karen matured a lot during the breakup. Their destiny together was reunited. Karen recalled feeling *optimistic,* believing that everything would work out. It was only the early days of their relationship, and Tom and Karen had their whole lives to look forward to. Karen opened up to Tom and told him that she *looked at life differently.*

"I feel I have a *more creative energy* that is not easy to express. I am *ready to tackle anything;* I feel so alive. I am ready to *dream the impossible,* and I *am open to whatever comes my way.* I trust my *intuition* to guide me, and I know soon enough I will find my place full of happiness and bliss.

Keywords/Phrases: Period of growth, fertile ground for new emotions, awakened feelings, optimistic, look at life differently, creative energy, dream the impossible, ready to tackle anything, open to whatever comes your way, intuition.

Further Interpretations: New love, artistic, an offer, a business proposition, a new project, early beginnings, immature, a reunion, social invitation, open-hearted, intimacy, optimistic, playful, exploration, innocence.

Visual Representation: The energy of the Page of Cups is almost always gentle and youthful. It portents to creativity and emotions, which can be used to identify an impressionable or emotional young person, child, or childlike adult. On this card, the Page stares into his cup, and surprisingly, a fish jumps out, revealing a vivid imagination and strong intuition. It says, "Dare to dream the impossible." Pages are often referred to as messengers, so you could also expect to receive a message that urges you to explore your emotional, creative self.

Knight of Cups

After declaring their love for each other, Tom and Karen settled back into a life full of joy. Who would have guessed that *dating* could be a full-time job? Tom made such an effort to win Karen back. He was her *knight in shining armour,* her *prince charming*. Their *love affair* moved fast. Emotions were high, and *romance was in the air*. Tom and Karen openly *declared their love for each other* and got back together. Karen recalled it being a great time. Tom was ever the *romantic, full of charm* and *in love with life*.

Karen recalled how Tom *swept her off her feet* with flowers and chocolates. He was so happy that Karen had changed her ways and accepted his job away from home. Karen remembered how much fun Tom was back then. He was so optimistic *and full of creative ideas*. He told Karen that he knew they would make it. He was going to make sure of it. Tom realised that his *love* for Karen was deeper than he could ever imagine, and he was not going to leave her again. They would work together and tackle every obstacle, speed bump, or detour. Tom was very *soft and sensitive* on the inside but could be a little rash and overenthusiastic on the surface. Both he and Karen had grown, and in some ways, their separation *healed* them.

Tom used his time away from Karen to get back *in tune with his feelings* and emotions. He was able to tap back into his *intuition* and listen to the guidance he received. Tom had a heart as big as the sea. He *shared his love freely* and was the maker of his dreams. With Karen once again by his side, he was able to *move forward.* Tom was on a mission to find peace from within his heart.

Keywords/Phrases: Knight in shining armour, prince charming, love affair, emotions are high, romance in the air, declared love, romantic, full of charm, in love with life, swept her off her feet, full of creative ideas, soft, sensitive, healed, in tune with his emotions and intuition, shares his love freely, moving forward.

Further Interpretations: Ruled by his heart, creative, artistic, a young man with an offer, a messenger or invitation resulting in emotional fulfilment, proposals, news of love, happy news coming your way, looks for perfection, romanticises.

Visual Representation: Remember, Cups are the suit of emotions. The Knight of Cups is looking to his emotions to provide a map. He is the person who is ruled by his heart rather than his head. He rides in with his heart (Cup) out in the open for all to see. When faced with a decision, he will always go with what his heart tells him, whether it is logical or not. He is a young man of high intelligence, a romantic dreamer. This card represents change and exciting news, particularly news that is romantic in nature. It is a card of invitations, opportunities, and offers. He is also refined and artistic, an amiable person but a dreamer.

Queen of Cups

Friends and family were relieved to hear that Karen and Tom were back together once again. They were very *emotionally intelligent* people and both had *deep empathy for others*, knowing instinctively what others were feeling before they said a word. They were *well-liked* because others could sense that *they cared*. Neither of them was *overdramatic*, and both were great role models for their friends and family. It was sad to see they had lost their way. Normally they were *even-tempered and emotionally strong*, and many of Karen's friends often told her she would make a great counsellor. People often confided in Karen because she had an *open and welcoming* aura about her. She was *very approachable*, and this was one of the things Tom loved about her. Karen was *warm* and had *the ability to work out problems diligently* before acting.

Life was good now that they were back together, and the couple happily rode its waves. Karen knew what she wanted and what she needed to get it. Tom always said that Gran would have loved her and that they would have been the best of friends. Karen had the same *ability to foresee things* she could not explain.

"*Your heart is your greatest strength*, Tom said one day, "but sometimes you give too much. You are the *most caring, kind, compassionate, and sensitive person* I know, and I love you deeply."

Karen knew she thought *predominately with her heart* and not her mind.

"When my heart was broken, I was lost," Karen said. "I, too, wish I had known your gran. I feel she talks to me. I have learned now how to listen and follow her guidance. Gran is part of me too. She reminds me to take care of myself so I can help, *teach*, and support others."

Keywords/Phrases: Emotionally intelligent, deep empathy for others, well-liked, caring, not over-dramatic, even-tempered, emotionally strong, worthy counsellor, open and welcoming, approachable, lovable, warm, ability to diligently work out problems, ability to foresee things, heart is her greatest strength, kind, compassionate, sensitive person, thinks with her heart.

Further Interpretations: Psychic, giving, follow your heart, love of home and family, understanding, gives unconditional love to all, nurturing, healing support, sometimes introverted, sensitive, cool-headed approach, self-respect.

Visual representation: The Queen of Cups is a happy card that represents balance and harmony. It also indicates success that is achieved due to a good imagination. The Queen keeps her emotions under control, is highly intuitive and psychic, and has a well-developed sixth sense. Her relationships are more mature than those of the Page or Knight. She is gentle, motherly, and a good listener. If you need a sympathetic ear and a shoulder to cry on, she is the one to seek out. The Queen will always offer practical and wise advice. Ever the romantic, she has a big heart and is forever nurturing, compassionate, and sensitive. This is Karen in a nutshell.

KING of CUPS.

King of Cups

Together, Tom and Karen's *vibrant energy* had expanded; however, Tom was the *power* behind the two. He was someone who *everyone could trust*. He had the ability to *bring the best out of other people*, and he was the *master of whatever he chose to do* in life. He was the *perfect husband* and a *great boss*. Tom had the *ability to accomplish many things* at once, which was rare for a man. Karen had never seen someone who was so *efficient at multi-tasking* like Tom. He was *warm* and *soft* but *very protective* of those he loved. He was a *seeker of love* and suffered the worst when he felt he could no longer handle Karen's insecurities early on in their relationship. Even though he was the one leaving, it broke his heart nonetheless.

Tom was a man who others sought out for relationship advice. He was said to be a *wise counsellor* for other people's pain. Karen used to say she was sure some of his customers at the store just came by to get Tom's opinion on something and purchased something as a cover-up. That never bothered Tom. He was always willing to listen and offer assistance.

If Tom said he was going to do something, you could be sure he would. He was definitely *a man of his word*, someone *you could count on.* Tony was very disappointed to see Tom leave his mechanic business because he was an exceptional employee. They had remained close friends though the years. Tom was the kind of man *who took relationships and close friendships very seriously.*

As a husband, Tom was the *master of romance* and treasured his and Karen's closeness. Over the course of their marriage, he never forgot a birthday or anniversary, often surprising Karen with amazing gifts. Karen remembered that on their tenth wedding anniversary, Tom hired a limousine to pick himself and Karen up from the store. They went to a fancy restaurant for dinner but not before he took her to the salon for a full makeover and the shops to purchase a new gown. Karen said she felt like royalty.

Keywords/Phrases: Powerful, someone everyone can trust, brings out the best in others, master of whatever he chooses, perfect husband, great boss, ability to accomplish many things, multi-tasker, warm, soft, protective, seeker of love, wise counsellor, man of his word, can be counted on, takes relationships and friendships seriously, master of romance.

Further Interpretations: Grounded, honourable, held in high regard, father figure, intelligent, knowledgeable, healer, empathy, a supportive leader.

Visual Representation: The King is the ultimate businessman who holds many responsible positions. He is in charge of his feelings and is able to remain in control of his emotions. The King of Cups in particular represents the balance between emotions and intellect. He is a master of compassion and kindness, and his actions are driven by the heart. He is a man of business and law and is kind, considerate, and willing to take responsibility. This is the type of man who commands respect, not love. He is empathetic, nurturing, and the essence of fatherly wisdom. He takes his relationships and friendships very seriously and is a man everyone can place their trust in.

IV

THE SWORDS

THE
SWORDS

"Nothing has any meaning except
the meaning you give it."
—Anthony Robbins

The Swords is the suit of the warrior. It deals with the mental level of consciousness, thought, and intellect. The Swords mirror the quality of mind present in our thoughts, attitudes, and beliefs and encompass how we communicate with others. Of all the suits, this one is often considered the most powerful. Swords equal worldly power and sometimes violence. They serve as a warning to watch where you are going and who you are dealing with. That way, you can use the sword to your advantage and change things for the better. Swords represent action, both constructive and destructive. Many of the cards in this suit illustrate fighting or states of misfortune. Swords can also trap you, especially your mind.

Ace of Swords

Over the previous few months, Karen had seen very little of Tom. He locked himself in his office from sunrise to well past sunset most days, diligently working on his *new* online *business*. He had comprised all his past *knowledge* and, with his *intellect and wisdom*, formulated a *new plan* to see his business venture succeed. He tried to stay *focused* and not become distracted by others.

With each passing day, Karen became more and more concerned. Tom was once again working himself to the bone.

He barely stopped to eat, and he was starting to look pale and drawn.

"I am constantly trying to get him outdoors more, but I know I am wasting my breath. Tom is obsessed," Karen told her mother.

Tom told Karen on one of their rare moments together that he finally felt like he was getting the hang of how the system worked.

"Finally," Karen said, feeling frustrated and annoyed. She knew Tom was not the type of man to just retire peacefully; he always had to have a purpose. But his new plans had a price.

Early one Sunday morning, Tom abruptly woke Karen up.

"I've got it!" he said.

Sitting up, rubbing sleep from her eyes, Karen asked, "What have you got?"

"I have this business all worked out," Tom said. "I've *had a moment of pure genius*. I don't know why I didn't think of this earlier. It is like that *light bulb moment* Gran often talked about. I have a clear plan now for what I am trying to achieve. I understand my limitations now and can focus my energies on what I know and am good at."

Tom sat down with Karen over breakfast and told her all about his *new ideas*. "I am thinking of taking on a partner, someone with computer skills who can help list all the parts I have been purchasing. This will free up my time so I can concentrate on the buying side of the business. I may even hire a team to handle the distribution." Tom knew this would impress Karen, as she had been on him every day to ease up a bit. He had found a way forward, and he was eager and determined to not allow any speed humps to deter him from his goal.

Karen and Tom had always shared common goals and operated on the same page. With them, it was like having two minds that worked as one. Tom knew Karen was just as excited as he was about the new business. He relied on her input and valued her opinions because he knew they made an unstoppable team. With this *aha moment*, Tom realized he had been a little overfocused lately and had shut Karen out, but with his *new insights*, life was about to change yet again. Tom had begun to look beyond what was in front of him and *see the bigger picture* of what he was trying to achieve.

Keywords/Phrases: New business, knowledge, intellect, wisdom, new plan, focused, moment of pure genius, light bulb moment, new ideas, aha moment, new insights, see the bigger picture.

Further Interpretation: Mental clarity, new strong cycle, strength of will, moment of genius, open communication. a gift, destiny, justice and fortitude.

Visual Representation: The hand of opportunity on the Ace of Swords card is offering Tom a new beginning or inspiration for a new idea. It represents the wondrous aha moments of life, the eruption of a new point of view, and the inspiration of discovery or intellectual accomplishment. With this card, there is a new understanding of some issue that has been of concern or the dawning of a new worldview. At this stage of life, Tom is experiencing moments of creative vision, keen intellect, and clarity of thought. The two-edged sword cuts deeply in both directions, and a fine line must be walked to achieve the balance necessary for a healthy life. This is a card of great power, breakthroughs, triumphs, victories, and new beginnings. Tom is being offered a gift.

Two of Swords

On this particular day, Tom decided he would skip breakfast, which he knew displeased Karen, but he was eager to get back to work. Tom started figuring out how he could restructure his business if he hired a partner. At first, the idea sounded like it had promise, but after further investigation, Tom was not so sure that it was the best solution. He was *conflicted* about what to do. He spent the next few days going over his figures and options. Where once Tom had clear thoughts about how he should structure his business, he was now faced with *two options* that both bid for his time and attention. The best thing he could do in this situation was sit quietly with his thoughts and *analyse which way he should go* and what he needed to do. Tom needed to allow himself the grace to slow down to think.

Tom's *mind was in turmoil.* He couldn't decide if he should go it alone, bring in a partner to train or bring in someone that did not need training at all. At this stage, he felt he *could not move forward.* Karen felt Tom's *anguish* and, as gently as possible, offered her advice on what she thought he should do. Tom was far too caught up in the *dilemma* to listen, so he once again closed himself off to Karen's thoughts. In his mind, her opinions were *clouding his judgment.* It wasn't like Tom to shut Karen out, and she let him know this in no uncertain terms.

"Just leave me alone for a bit to *think this out,*" he said.

"Open your eyes; you are *blinded by your own fear* and control. This is not a hard decision," Karen replied. Regardless, she trusted Tom to make the right decision on his own, but she was not happy that he was *overthinking* everything and shutting her out.

Tom wanted to trust reason, and he knew he was struggling on his own. But for some reason, he was in a *state of analysis paralysis, a complete standstill, a stalemate.* He knew he couldn't move forward until he made *a decision.* Tom had avoided asking for help up until this point, and he was exhausted from trying to do it all on his own. This placed unnecessary stress on himself and his family. He felt like his *heart was in conflict with his thoughts.* He told Karen one day that it felt like he was caught between a rock and a hard place. Tom knew he couldn't stay between *two minds* forever; a decision had to be made sooner rather than later, for everyone's sake. He would've loved nothing more than to be able to do it all on his own, but deep down, he knew it was time to make a *wise, intuitive decision;* he had to get help.

During Tom's time in *quiet contemplation*, he had come to realize that he could achieve more if he focused solely on one thing within the structure of his business rather than trying to achieve everything on his own. There was so much to learn and do, and he was only one man.

Keywords/Phrases: Conflict, two options, analyse which way to go, mind in turmoil, cannot decide, cannot move forward, anguish, dilemma, clouding his judgment, think this out, blinded by fear, overthinking, analysis paralysis, a decision, heart in conflict with thoughts, of two minds, wise and intuitive decision, quiet contemplation.

Further Interpretations: Let me think, working everything out internally, find a compromise, make a decision, mental anguish, a solution needs to be found, a stalemate, consideration needed, processing next move.

Visual Representation: With the Two of Swords, Tom has some big decisions to make, but unless he removes his blindfold, he will remain in a state of paralysis and procrastination. There will be no win or loss. Life's decisions are frequently quite difficult and can raise the possibility of painful consequences, but not deciding at all is a decision in itself. The avoidance will ultimately lead to greater conflict in the end. Tom must open his eyes and make decisions with the best intentions, fully aware of the possible consequences. This is a card of choice, of the difficulty of indecision. The past is on its way out, and a new element is about to emerge that will make the old way obsolete. Occasionally, when we are faced with difficult choices, we attempt to hide from them and pretend that if we ignore them long enough, they will go away on their own. However, the decision will not leave us because of our desire for it to depart; ignorance is not always bliss. Our conscience will eventually force us to face our refusal to deal with the situation directly.

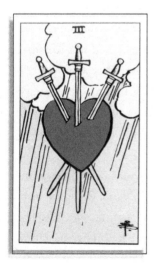

Three of Swords

A few days later, Tom told Karen over breakfast that he was not feeling his best. She suggested he take the day off to rest, and she even offered to cook his favourite chicken soup, a recipe from his dear Gran. But as the day progressed, Tom began to feel worse. It was around 2:00 p.m. when Karen left Tom asleep on the couch to go outside and collect the mail. On entering through the kitchen door, Karen glanced in on Tom to check if he was still sleeping. She was shocked to find him sitting up, clutching his chest. Instantly, she knew something was not right and called for an ambulance. The paramedics arrived within ten minutes, and they took one look at Tom and told the couple he was going straight to the hospital. Karen rode along in the ambulance and called Isac and Alice on the way to ask them to meet her at the hospital.

Sadly, all the long hours and *neglect* that Tom had placed on himself had finally landed him in hospital. Tom had not eaten a full meal or slept through an entire night since he started his new venture. Many nights, Tom often woke at 4:00 a.m. to walk the halls. Sometimes he would sit out on the veranda if it was a warm night and just think. He never came back to bed but instead dozed off outside until the morning light woke him. The new business was causing Tom so much *stress and literal heartache.*

Learning new skills was becoming harder than Tom expected at his older age, and having to stay in the hospital hit him hard. After the doctors examined him, they told Karen that Tom had suffered a mild heart attack and was to remain in the hospital overnight for observation. They assured her he would be fine with some rest. Lately, Karen had felt betrayed and abandoned by her husband. She knew he had to change his ways or he could end up right back in the hospital again—and next time, it could be much more serious.

After the doctor left, Karen gave Tom a piece of her mind. He sat quietly in the bed, not saying a word. She gave him a kiss and told him to get some rest and that she would be back in the morning to bring him home. That had been a bit of a wake-up call for Tom, one that was long overdue. Tom recalled something his Gran would say: "We cannot resist pain; we must recognize it. *Understanding your pain can set you on the path toward healing.* Your mind, heart, and body are all connected; abuse one, and you abuse them all." Gran was never wrong. Tom reprimanded himself for not listening to her.

That night in the hospital, Tom got very little sleep. He admitted to himself that he had been neglecting his family, and tension had been mounting between himself and Karen for some time. With this realization, he felt slightly *relieved*. His heart attack, while unpleasant and scary, was in some small way necessary. Tom could finally see the part he played in his demise and self-destruction. He had come to realize that his blindness and self-delusion could not go on. He had been *suppressing his emotions*, and he knew that sooner or later they had to come out, and they did. Luckily, his heart attack was not severe, but it was still frightening.

The next morning, Karen and the kids grabbed a quick bite to eat and raced out the door, eager to get back to the hospital to see Tom. They arrived and were pleased to see him sitting up, attempting to eat breakfast. After the kids left, Karen pulled a chair close to Tom's bed and took him by the hand.

"You gave me such a fright," she said. "I have never been so worried in all my life. You are my world, you know that? And I hope this has been *a huge eye-opener* for you. It is time to come home. You have been missing, not so much physically but mentally and spiritually, for too long. It is time to face that this new business is causing you too much anxiety and stress. You have to slow down, Tom. *You need to communicate* what you are going through instead of keeping it all bottled up like you did when we were at the store. I am here to help you, so please use me; don't push me away."

Tom sat in silence with his head hung low. He looked up at his beautiful wife and promised to *change his ways* when he got back home. Tom felt an *enormous release* from all the *self-inflicted pressure* he had placed upon himself. He faced up to all the *pain and demands* he, and only he, had caused.

Keywords/Phrases: Neglect, stress, heartache, understanding your pain, set the path to healing, relieved, suppressing emotions, a huge eye-opener, a need to communicate, change your ways, enormous relief, self-inflicted pressure, pain, demands.

Further Interpretations: It's over, see the truth, what a relief, problems are now out in the open, time to heal, end of suffering, negative thinking, a huge release.

Visual Representation: Just looking at this card, you know something painful has happened or surfaced from the past. But from the pain and the experience, something far greater will infold. To move forward and allow the healing process to begin, you must face this pain head-on. Tom's heart attack was a huge wake-up call for him. New ideas or actions must replace the old ones, and something better will be established that could not have happened without the painful situation. This pain and its cause need to be taken care of before Tom can go on.

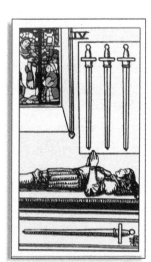

Four of Swords

Returning back home after Tom's health scare, Karen decided it was time to *take a break.*

"Sometimes, in life, everything seems to pile up and get the best of us," she said to Tom. "The best cure for this is *to break away from the troubles and pressure* of everyday life. You must take a *few steps back*, even if just for a while, and *let go*, or you will end up right back in the hospital again."

Karen booked a few nights at their favourite Airbnb, not far from their home. They arrived later the next day and settled in before heading out on the town for dinner. They had a lovely night together, something they both had missed.

The next morning, they went to the beach for a beautiful walk and to catch a bit of sun before lunch. Together, they laid on the beach in peaceful silence, with only the sounds of the waves crashing on the shore and the seagulls squawking overhead. Tom closed his eyes and became lost in his thoughts. This time of *quiet contemplation, reflection, rest, and retreat* soothed his heart and mind. His confusion and anguish dissipated, and he felt alive once again. He thought of his gran and knew she was smiling down on him.

"In stillness, you will receive. Let your mind be still, for from the silent pause comes some of our most amazing thoughts. The universe has ways of forcing us to stop and listen," Gran would say to Tom. "You will often feel worse until you come to recognise *the need for silence and introversion.*

Stillness and quiet time are often needed to know where you're going; otherwise, you'll end up going around in circles."

Karen was pleased to see Tom relaxing and enjoying himself. Later that afternoon, he told her he was going for a walk alone. That was fine with Karen, as she had plans to spend the afternoon down by the pool with the new novel she'd purchased at the store on the way back from the beach that morning.

Tom needed *time alone* with his thoughts to figure out where to go next. The weekend away was just what he needed to *sort out his priorities*. He was beginning *to let go, relax, and release* all the tensions of the past. He thought of all the changes he was going to make in his life when he got back home, marshalling up the strength and inner reserves to carry on his business. But this time, he would do so in a much more controlled sense. He examined the patterns that caused his demise and vowed to never fall prey to that kind of hardship again. Tom had never valued quiet and stillness in the past, but now he moved his focus off the big picture to attend to all the little things that had been piling up. He was now aware that *introspection* had its benefits, as rushing from one thing to another did not cure or help anything. *Stillness* was needed if he was going to succeed.

Keywords/Phrases: Take a rest, respite away from troubles and pressure, step back, let go, quiet contemplation, reflection, time-out, retreat, a need for silence and introversion, stillness and quiet, time alone, sort out priorities, relax, release, introspection.

Further Interpretations: Meditation, mental stability, withdraw, stable mind, step back, make time for yourself, rest after strife, solitude, recovery, healing, recuperation, conflict resolution.

Visual representation: Lay your negative thoughts or problems aside and give yourself time to clear your head and find purpose before continuing on. It is time for solitude so you can gather your thoughts and feelings apart from others. Following the pain experienced with the Three of Swords, the Four of Swords indicates that it's time to be alone and re-evaluate our lives and situations. Solitude, although often difficult to bear, is exactly what Tom needed to "recharge his batteries" and rejuvenate his spirit. Now the healing can begin.

Five of Swords

Returning home from their wonderful weekend away, Karen felt like Tom still had a lot to learn. It seemed like their getaway did little to tame his flames. Tom was still obsessed and was back in his office working harder than ever. He clearly struggled to let go, and Karen often told him that if he didn't change, he'd have to face losing her or ending up back in the hospital.

Their once beautiful home was full of *tension and negative energy.* Tom rarely sat at the dinner table to eat, preferring instead to eat on the run or go without. Karen refused to bring his meals into his office and had even stopped cooking for him altogether. Because of the negative energy, Karen hated being at home and found herself spending more and more time away. Tom had overstepped his boundaries and was trying to achieve something beyond his abilities. He wouldn't see reason and lost sight of why he had started the business in the first place. Karen, on the other hand, was tired of the same old *arguments* that went around and around and never seemed to get resolved.

One day, Tom refused to help Karen move the outdoor setting in the garden, claiming he was just too busy. That was the straw that broke the camel's back. They had a massive argument, right there in the backyard, the worse they'd had in their twenty years of marriage. Thankfully, the kids were not home to hear them yelling back and forth. Neither of them listened to what the other was saying. Karen thought Tom had become unbearable to live with and felt *defeated and rejected.* After being talked over and dismissed time and time again, she threw her hands in the air and walked away, leaving Tom *with the impression he had won, but sadly he was losing.*

If only he could see that his "my way or the highway" attitude was getting him nowhere. Tom's *attitude and intimidation* worked against him as he tried to *dominate* Karen and gain his own self-worth. Tom used *trickery, deceit, and unfair tactics* to try and win the argument. Their marriage was suffering severely, and Tom needed to *change his ways* before it was too late.

Tom's intimidation and clever *manipulation* were not lost on Karen. She was aware of his ways but nonetheless backed down for her own sanity. "Let him think he is the king," she mumbled to herself. He may have thought he had the upper hand, but he had actually *lost* Karen's *respect* and support. The two of them had seemingly *lost their connection* with one another, and as such, they were experiencing a huge *communication breakdown*.

Later that night, Tom stewed in his office, clearly feeling quite upset. He couldn't concentrate on anything; his head was all screwed up. He felt remorse for the way he'd spoken to Karen earlier that day, and he worried that he and Karen were *not working together* like they had in the past. Tom sat in silence for a while before realizing that he must swallow his pride and apologise to his wife. He had said some hurtful things that he now regretted. Tom faced the fact that he had been rather piggish about the whole thing, and he knew he had been acting selfishly. There would be no real resolution unless he began to accept Karen's wishes and listen to what she had to say.

Keywords/Phrases: Attitude, intimidation, dominate, trickery, deceit, unfair tactics, change his ways, manipulation, lost respect, lost connection, communication breakdown, not working together.

Further Interpretations: Won the war, lost the battle, win but no gain, negative energy, change communication, keep the barriers up, bullies, conflicting situation, arguments and hassles, volatile, drama, conflict, fear of defeat, tension, integrity.

Visual Representation: Look at the big picture and the role you are playing. Are you the callous winner or the dejected loser? You may feel smug and pleased with what you are achieving, but are you stepping on others' toes and causing chaos and conflict within your life that you are not even aware of? In any case, the Five of Swords has a general negative connotation. It is time for Tom to think of the "we", not just the "me". If your focus is solely on achieving your goals at any cost, you will eventually discover, to your own dismay, that the price of winning may not have been worth the reward. Tom is about to discover just that.

Six of Swords

Tom had lost sight of himself and his reasons behind starting the new business. He knew it was time to get help before he lost everything he had worked so hard to achieve— if not for his health's sake, at least for the sake of his marriage. Tom resigned himself to the fact that it was time to apologise to Karen. He knew he must also get serious about delegating some of the work-load. Sitting at his desk, Tom felt a flash of insight, the first he'd had in a long time. All the *pain and strife* he felt gave way to *calm and clarity*. He was ready to surrender and admit defeat. Tom had come to his senses and was prepared to accept his limitations. All the difficulties he'd faced over the last few months had taken their toll on his sanity. He was ready to *move forward* to a more peaceful mindset. He was happy to *leave behind the anxious, distressing, and troubled times*.

After dinner, Tom and Karen had a good heart-to-heart and vowed to put *the past behind them*. Tom apologised for the hurtful things he said and for putting his marriage in jeopardy. It was a *new day* and all their *worries were put to rest*. Tom breathed a sigh of relief and began to make new plans to bring in a business partner who could help with the workload. Karen was happy that Tom was starting to see things more objectively and clearly. She knew there would be *better days ahead*.

A new day was dawning, and the couple felt optimistic about their future. Finally, they were back on the same page, working side by side. They could *move forward* once again as a team. Happiness had not quite returned, but a harmonious feeling was slowly emerging from the darkness of the *tense past few months*. Tom had said some very hurtful things to Karen that were uncalled for, and she was having a hard time forgetting. She forgave him because it was all said in the heat of the argument, but it was painful nonetheless. She knew she would eventually get over it; she could forgive but would never forget.

Tom's new spark of ingenuity soothed the storm clouds in his mind, and *life was once again sailing along nicely*. He had changed his working hours so he was at the table every night for dinner, and *peace was finally restored* in the house. Tom and Karen put their *troubles behind them* and felt optimistic that there would be *better times ahead*. Tom's business was progressing as planned, and he felt like there was a *light at the end of the tunnel*. All his hard work would soon pay off, as he accepted his limitations.

The love between Tom and Karen gradually resurfaced, and Tom was beginning to look at their relationship in *a whole new light*. He admitted he had nothing without her. Karen was the backbone of their marriage. She was the glue that held it all together. *What on earth was I thinking?* he thought to himself. He was ashamed of his past behaviour and was grateful to Karen for giving him yet another chance.

Keywords/Phrases: From pain and strife to calm and clarity; ready to move forward; leave behind the anxious, distressing, troubled times; new day; worries are put to rest; better days ahead; move forward; tense past; life is sailing along nicely; peace finally restored; troubles are behind them; light at the end of the tunnel;

Further Interpretations: Your back is to the trauma, smooth sailing, travel, relocation, regroup, move from conflict, easy transitions, mental peace after trouble and strife, letting go, you have the support you need.

Visual Representation: Thank God that is over and life can move forward trouble-free. The sadness felt from the loss or hard times of the Five of Swords will ultimately be replaced by greater clarity. This is represented on the card by the calmness of the water in the distance, which will bring about a new understanding and acceptance of the changes in our lives. The Six of Swords represents a time of peace and relaxation after a long struggle. Tom and Karen are resurfacing out of a difficult experience with the wisdom to know they cannot dwell on the past. This card symbolises gradual change as well as movement from eminent danger and immediate difficulties. This is a positive direction to go in. Regroup and move forward.

Seven of Swords

Life went on peacefully for the couple for a few months, and both of them were beginning to reclaim their faith in each other. Karen had always loved and supported Tom throughout their twenty years of marriage. She had covered his back on more than one occasion. "Till death do us part, in sickness and in health," but Karen was finally at the end of her tether. This time, Tom had crossed the line.

During her trip into town for groceries, Karen ran into their bank manager, who cautiously asked Karen if everything was all right with Tom. Karen assured him that everything was fine but asked why he seemed so concerned. He told Karen that Tom's business account was overdrawn and that it might be a good time for them to make an appointment to see if he could be of any help.

Tom's obsession with his business had pushed Karen to her breaking point. She rushed home to confront him with their bank statements in hand. Karen was an excellent bookkeeper and was disappointed in herself for not spotting this sooner. When she last did the monthly accounts, there were ample funds available. So, what had Tom been up to that would overdraw their account? Trying to keep her temper from exploding on the drive home, she turned on the radio to distract her overreacting mind and keep her cool. When she got home, she stood outside of Tom's office for a while to compose herself, taking a deep breath before entering.

Karen tossed the bank statements on his desk and asked him to explain all his spending. She told him how embarrassed she felt by their bank manager telling her their account was in arrears. Tom tried to explain that he had purchased some new stock and was waiting for the sales to come in. He was expecting the sales any day now, and the account would be in the black soon. He tried his best to assure Karen that everything was all right, and he asked her not to worry because he had everything under control. Karen knew her husband well and was convinced he was *lying* to her. It would not surprise her if he was *deceiving* her. His obsession had brought about *secretiveness and dishonesty*.

Karen wanted to know why he did not tell her about the purchases sooner. She could have rearranged their accounts to cover the costs without overdrawing. Tom fumbled with his words, full of excuses. *What is he hiding?* Karen thought. Tom acted nonchalantly, as if nothing was wrong, hoping Karen would drop the subject and let him get away with his *deceit.* This time, though, Karen was not backing down. Tom needed to take a good long look at himself before he lost everything he'd worked so hard for.

"It would be *best to stop, take stock*, and make sure this is what you really want," Karen said, finishing the conversation. "If it is, then I'm *leaving*. If it isn't, now is the time to reconsider your ways."

Keywords/Phrases: Lying, secretive, dishonesty, deceit, stop and take stock, leaving, walking away.

Further Interpretations: Theft, betrayal, dishonesty, be cautious, more than meets the eye, something underhanded going on behind your back, need to be alert and on guard, tricky situation, cunning strategies, flies under the radar, manipulative.

Visual Representation: There are times in life when it is necessary to act shrewdly or in secret, yet it is these times when our conscience must be particularly active. In the long run, deception often does not produce the rewards we desired, and we may in fact cause damage to our relationships and reputation in the process. Tom struggles with conformity and is playing the victim all too well. Sometimes we have to face what's necessary and use caution and circumspection when attempting to gain a potentially unfair advantage. Are you running from something, procrastinating, or letting problems slip because you don't want to deal with them? Sometimes we must face these issues head-on.

Eight of Swords

Tom had been holding Karen off for too long. He once again *felt stuck, trapped*, and unsure why he had been acting so unlike himself. He had to make a choice and commit to either their marriage or his business, but he was *paralysed by the fear* of losing both. Tom had been *in denial* and was shocked that his subterfuges and sneaky tactics had come to this point. He had been blinded by his own *self-sabotaging* actions, believing he must do everything himself to prove that he was good enough to Karen and others. Tom's thoughts and beliefs were no longer serving him. It was too late for regrets; he knew the mess was all in his making. He had to accept responsibility for his actions and act once and for all if there was ever going to be hope for Karen and Tom's future.

Tom tried to tell Karen that he believed he had no alternative but to deceive her. "I must succeed at all costs," he said. "I have *lost all my power,* and it is as if this business has *taken all my strength.* I have *lost my way* and no longer have the *courage* to fight it. I can't go on. I surrender." Tom faced the radical acceptance that it has *all become too much.* Tom pleaded for Karen to understand. "I *feel frustrated* that whatever way I turn, I am faced with problems." This behaviour was so unlike the "get it done" Tom she knew and loved. It was very rare for him to throw his hands in the air and *admit defeat.* She told him to pick himself up and dust himself off.

"Stop feeling sorry for yourself. You got this. Get out of your head. Stop putting so much pressure on yourself. You are your *own worst enemy.*"

Karen left Tom to think long and hard about his behaviour and got herself ready for bed. It was well past midnight when Tom finally came in. He had been sitting alone in the dark, lost in his thoughts. He realized he had caused the whole dilemma with his avoidance, blindness, and fear. He had been *playing the victim,* and his business was his enemy. He realized that no one was challenging him to be a success, least of all Karen. Tom had already proved himself to her on many occasions. Still, he *felt trapped* by his *lack of confidence* and felt that changing the situation was beyond his control. Tom drifted off to sleep, thinking that if only he could *let go of control, get out of his head,* and *commit to changing,* he could save his marriage and business.

The wall of stone Tom had placed around himself was of *his own doing.* He knew he was the only one who could defeat it. Karen was right; he needed *to take the pressure off of himself.*

"If the business fails, then it fails. I am no less of a man for trying. But I will do my best to not allow that to happen. It's time to step up and commit to changing my circumstances. Just like Gran would say, '*You reap what you sow.*'"

Keywords/Phrases: Feeling stuck, trapped, paralysed by fear, in denial, self-sabotage, lost power, taken my strength, lost my way, courage, surrender, all becomes too much, feel frustrated, throw hands in the air, admit defeat, own worst enemy, playing the victim, lack of confidence, let go of control, get out of your head, commit to change, own doing, take the pressure off, reap what you sow.

Further Interpretations: Self-imposed restrictions, isolation, imprisonment, illusions, self-sabotage, bound up, believe in yourself, limiting beliefs, gripped by fear, a no-win situation, dammed if you do/dammed if you don't, radical acceptance.

Visual Representation: This card represents feeling fenced in, restricted, and vulnerable with no direction. With the Eight of Swords, though, all of these feelings are being invented within your mind and are not real. Your hands may be tied, but your legs are not, and the blindfold can be removed easily at any time. You could open your eyes and walk away if you choose. Realize that you are not trapped, that you are free to move and change your circumstances. It may seem like you are stuck, and it can be hard to see what to do, but if you simply reach out your hand, you'll find that the swords are nearby and can be used to cut yourself free. It's your call. Time for Tom to step up.

Nine of Swords

Tom laid in bed and stared at the ceiling, trying not to disturb Karen. His head was a mess, and *sleep eluded him*. He tried to remain calm, but his *worries and anxieties* enveloped him. He *tossed and turned* and finally got up, knowing he was *not going to sleep tonight*. Tom turned things over and over in his mind, from his *past troubles* to *his present problems* to his grim visions of the future. He was slowly falling into a state of *deep depression* and couldn't seem to find his way out. He was racked with *shame and guilt* about how he had handled everything. The pressure he had put himself under caused him to have a mild *panic attack*, and he began to feel scared.

Tom's behaviour and obsessiveness over his business had plunged himself and Karen into debt. That was not at all what he intended. His mind thought of all the consequences debt entailed, and he had visions of them losing their home, becoming bankrupt, and living on the streets. Tom couldn't shake the gloom he felt. He began to worry for his kids' futures because if money became tight, so would their education. Tom *overanalysed* every decision he'd made, bringing up even more *fears and worries*. Karen would probably tell him he was making a *mountain out of a molehill*, and maybe he was. But he felt the pain nonetheless.

Tom wandered out to the veranda to sit for a while. He took a few deep breaths and began to relax a little. If Karen should wake and find him missing, she would begin to worry and that was something he wanted to avoid. The whole situation was causing him to sink deeper and deeper into a life of darkness. He refused to ask for help, and he was struggling to remain positive. A small part of Tom whispered, "Things won't seem so hopeless in the light of day. You will be OK. You'll find the way; you always have."

Tom thought of what Gran would say and sat silently, listening to the night birds and crickets. He felt Gran's presence with him and calmed down even more. "*It's all in your head,* boy," he swore he heard her say. "Stop playing the victim and *change your thoughts*. Think of all the good in your life instead of all this negativity. You are *bringing this doom upon yourself.*"

Tom sat stunned by this voice, sure that it was coming from outside of himself. "All that is happening is from your own imagination. Go back to bed," he heard the voice say. With that, Tom got up and silently climbed back in bed beside Karen, immediately drifting off to sleep. The next morning, he struggled to get up. He was on the verge of tears. He wandered around in a zombie-like state for days, and Karen was beginning to worry once again.

Keywords/Phrases: Sleep eluded him, worries, anxieties, tossed and turned, not going to sleep, past troubles, present problems, deep depression, shame and guilt, panic attack, worries, over-analysing everything, fear, making a mountain out of a molehill, it is all in your head, change your thoughts, bringing doom upon yourself.

Further Interpretations: Nervous breakdown, sleepless nights, nightmares, overthinking, playing the martyr, self-critical.

Visual Representation: The Nine of Swords reminds us that we are the creators of our world, and our attitudes determine how we experience that world. Our fears, negative thoughts, and troubles are primarily of a psychological nature and do not necessarily indicate suffering in our external reality. Our experience of the world is greatly influenced by our expectations, desires, and fears. If Tom allows himself to be bound by a fear of the future, he may eventually create a negative reality for himself by virtue of his expectations. He may worry more about problems that never would have bothered him in the past, causing him to lay awake at night, overthink, and create bigger problems for himself. When this card shows up, it's time to face the truth that this mental turmoil is only happening in your head.

Ten of Swords

Finally, the inevitable happened. Tom's doubts and lack of faith in himself sent him plummeting into despair and a deep depression. Karen had never seen him so despondent.

"*There's nothing more to say, nothing more to think about.* I have failed you and the kids," Tom said to Karen. He had hit rock bottom, and he felt like his life was in shambles. He had lost sight of where he was going. Every way he looked he faced another brick wall. He was *struggling mentally*, and Karen felt that it was time for him to seek help. He wouldn't talk with her, and she was tired of trying.

He had *reached the end*; he was at the *point of no return.* He no longer knew who he was or where he was going. *How on earth did I allow this to get this far?* Karen thought to herself. She felt so disappointed in not just Tom but herself. *I should have seen this coming months ago.* Karen tried hard to not fall. She had to remain strong for the both of them.

Tom's past behaviour of neglect and obsession had finally caught up with him, and he *collapsed*. He spent the night on the couch huddled close to his *empty* scotch bottle. That was where Karen found him the next morning, still in his clothes from the day before. He looked a wreck; he hadn't shaved in at least a week, and his eyes were completely *lifeless*.

Karen sat next to Tom in silence, lost for what to say. He looked up at and said, "I feel like I have been to hell and back."

"You sure look like it," Karen said with a slight smile. She did her best to reassure him that things couldn't get any worse, that there was still hope. She tried to make light of the situation.

After months of a repetitive cycle, Tom's obsession was over. He had hit the wall. He was *done, cooked, finished*. Karen was sad it had to come to this, but Tom's *breakdown* was inevitable. Even his heart attack was not enough for him to see sense. Karen reminded Tom of what his gran would say at a time like this: "Know when to fold your cards, boy. Find the beauty in the lesson and move on. Stop holding on to what must die. Let whatever isn't working in your life go so something better can take its place. You are about to be reborn if you can get out of your own way."

Karen got up to make herself and Tom a cup of coffee. They moved outside to the veranda to sit in the sun. Tom told Karen how much he had missed her and how sorry he felt for the pain he caused. They both began to cry tears of sadness and love. They hugged each other tightly and vowed to never shut the other out again. After a while, they began to feel a sense of hope arise within them. As they separated and took deep breaths, Tom wondered what the next step was. Suddenly, he sprung to his feet, smiling down at a very surprised Karen.

"I've got an idea!"

Keywords/Phrases: There is nothing more to say, nothing more to think about, hit rock bottom, struggling mentally, reach the end, point of no return, collapse, lifeless, empty, a wreck, things cannot get any worse, done, cooked, finished, breakdown.

Further Interpretations: Painful ending, end of stressful conditions after many trials and tribulations, death of an old cycle, cannot get any worse, the end, the beginning, new opportunities for happiness will appear, the worst is over, a great sense of relief, epiphany, steps to freedom, change the way you think.

Visual Representation: You cannot die twice. The worst has happened, and now Tom can pick himself up and move on. Though the Ten of Swords may seem negative at first glance, it is a card of hope and an indication that your troubles will not be permanent. There is finally closure to an outstanding issue, which may have been difficult and resulted in endings and loss. But as with all endings, there is a new beginning, a rebirth, and a rejuvenation of the spirit right around the corner. The process of change is often difficult, yet life is filled with uncertainty. The only thing that's constant in life is change! So, welcome it.

Page of Swords

Tom's sudden *flash of insight* brought him back to life. Karen was once again relieved to have her old Tom back to his usual, happy self. Tom was a *thinker and a planner*, along with having a *brilliant mind*. As a child, his mother said he was often thought to be *a genius*, a handful but a little genius nonetheless. He was a curious child. Karen could see those same traits within the man she married. Tom used to love tinkering in the back garden shed, inventing all sorts of gadgets. He could break a motor down to one thousand pieces and know exactly where each part belonged to put it back together.

Tom had *brand-new plans* for his and Karen's future, but it was only the *early days,* and this time he would not hesitate to ask for assistance. He had been *brainstorming the new idea* for weeks, but he held off on telling Karen until he had everything mapped out. Tom's mind would never rest; he accepted this. He was not happy if he wasn't planning or organising something.

Tom still had a lot more *learning and study* to do before he was ready to formulate his ideas and present his concepts to Karen. She knew Tom well and often made sure to be the grounding force he needed to come back down to Earth. Tom had a tendency to let his mind carry him away.

Over dinner, Karen reminded Tom of what his gran used to say to him whenever his mind ran off with him: "Keep it simple, and you will win the game of life." Tom assured Karen that was exactly what he was doing.

Keywords/Phrases: Flash of insight, thinker and planner, brilliant mind, genius, brand-new plans, early days, brainstorming new ideas, learning and study.

Further Interpretations: Curiosity, an exciting new challenge, truthful, analytical, researcher, learning something new, relies on logic and reason, battles are looming, get ready to fight, new focus, seeds planted.

Visual Representation: In the essence of youth, having fun with mental activities of all kinds, whether it's learning, exploring, or researching. Opening your mind to far greater thought processes. This Page reminds Tom to appreciate and communicate his ideas, information, and theories. Tom is the page here looking off into the distance, thinking, *What can I learn today?*

KNIGHT OF SWORDS

Knight of Swords

Karen shook her head at Tom. "You can't fool me," she said. When Tom put his *mind to something*, it was *full steam ahead*. Thankfully, Karen trusted Tom enough to know he had learned from his past mistakes, but still, she warned him against *rushing in too quickly*. His plans were coming along fast, but this time, Tom was *full of confidence* and assured Karen that he would meet any problems head on before they escalated.

Karen was beyond happy to see Tom full of enthusiasm once again. Never one to remain idle for long, he preferred to keep himself busy, but this sometimes caused him to be *too eager and rush into ideas* before he was certain where he was going. Tom's mind had a tendency to leap from one thing to another, and Karen often struggled to keep up him. This adventurous quality is what Karen most admired about Tom. There was never a dull moment with him. Tom enjoyed the *quest of knowledge* but would generally become bored before he had the chance to master the task, moving on to something shinier and newer.

Karen tried not to worry too much about Tom, but it was not long before he threw ordinary life into disorder once again. This time, though, he moved through the turbulence he created with decisiveness and confidence. While Tom knew he must *act quickly* if his new plans were to take off, he had not yet learned how to not act impulsively. Tom had the greatest ability of accomplishing many things at the same time, which Karen joked about often, referring to Tom as the male *multitasker*. Tom had *many opinions*, but he was also a *revolutionist*.

Karen had learned over the course of her and Tom's marriage to not try and give Tom orders. Tom *disliked being told what to do* and would refuse or do the opposite, even if he had plans to do it beforehand. Karen always let Tom think things were his idea first. She simply planted the seed and let Tom's independent mind do the rest. They really did have a special partnership.

Keywords/Phrases: Full steam ahead, rushing in too quickly, full of confidence, too eager, hurrying ideas along, quest for knowledge, act quickly, multitasker, dislikes being told what to do.

Further Interpretations: Not enough thought, time for swift action, focused, fast talker, truth is your weapon, opinionated, revolutionist.

Visual Representation: When the Knight gets an idea, he is off to the races. He is on a mission, and nothing can slow him down. His trusty steed barely has time to put four feet on the ground. He believes that actions speak louder than words. When storms are approaching, he is able to hop on his horse and ride directly into the wind. He is fearless and will move forward against all odds.

Queen of Swords

One afternoon while sitting outside with a cold beer, Tom's thoughts drifted to Karen. He loved the way she mixed wisdom with humour. Karen also had a *brilliant mind* and was a strong match for Tom. When things turn topsy turvey, as it often did in their household, Tom could always count on Karen to remain *cool, calm, and collected.* She was *soft-hearted* but could *cut straight to the bone* if she had to. Karen had the ability to cut though the bullshit and see the truth in life.

Karen's *wit and class* went a long way and was admired by all who knew her. She *stood her ground* and was *not easy to push around.* She knew what she wanted and was very *self-reliant,* never overly concerned by what others thought of her. She did what she wanted when she wanted. She was a smart, *independent, strong,* and an extremely *classy* lady. She always knew what to say, and because of that, they had so many friends. She was *also a shrewd judge of character,* and Tom often relied on her judgment. What Tom loved most about Karen was that she never beat around the bush. She always said it like it was, *a straight shooter,* a trait she inherited from her parents.

Karen had experienced life's many ups and downs, and her strength, knowledge, and experience were sought after by others. Karen freely offered her help to anyone in need. She was not afraid to hurt someone's feelings and preferred to be *direct* and *to the point* with her advice, which was often much appreciated. She had a way of demanding people's respect and admiration. Karen was a *great communicator* and had a way of helping others think for themselves and explore new ideas with a clear head and intellectual understanding. Over the course of their marriage, Tom had become well-aware of Karen's ability to plant seeds of ideas in his head.

Tom thought back to the time when the competitor's store opened down the road. Karen was the first person in the door to check it out. If she was ever upset about something, she would think her emotions through. She rarely lost her cool or flew off the handle, but when she did, you would be better off to stand back. She was rarely merciful in those moments, and Tom knew all too well that if Karen was giving him a talking to, she had thought about her words thoroughly before bringing the subject to his attention. Karen always *spoke the truth*, no matter if you wanted to hear it or not. She was a *professional mediator*, which was a great trait to have when a customer complained at the store. She had a way of talking to people that soothed and settled them. Tom knew he was nothing without her. Karen was his rock.

Keywords/Phrases: Brilliant mind, cool, calm, collected, soft-hearted, cut straight to the bone, wit and class, stands her ground, not easy to push around, smart, independent, strong, shrewd judge of character, a straight shooter, direct and to the point, great communicator, speaks the truth, pro meditator.

Further Interpretations: Witty, insightful, good sense of humour, self-reliant, powerful, trustworthy, fashionable, cuts through BS.

Visual Representation: The Queen of Swords always remains cool in a crisis. She sits on her throne with her sword held erect to show she is unbiased in her opinions. She has the maturity and intellect to solve problems without clouding her judgment with emotions. She is a seeker of truth and prefers to get right to the point. Not to be messed with.

King of Swords

KING of SWORDS.

If you thought Karen was a force to be reckoned with, then you must understand that Tom was *no pushover* either. He had an *air of authority* about him and was a *man of his word.* He may not stick with it in the long term, but he would definitely get the job done. Tom's presence alone *commanded great respect* from his friends and employees. He'd never ask anyone to do something he couldn't do himself. He was known to be a very *fair and just* man, but at times, he could be quite *critical and judgmental.* He could sometimes come across as harsh or like an *iron-fist tyrant.* Tom just liked to get the job done with no fluff.

With that said, Tom was the most *brilliant and inventive* man Karen had ever known. She'd had the opportunity to witness Tom grow and mature over the years. Where once he would rush in without thinking things through, he now took careful consideration in all matters before he acted. He was *highly intelligent* and destiny made sure he was a leader of others and his own boss. He was a *man of authority.* There's a fine line between insane and genius, and at times Karen wished Tom was a little softer and affectionate, but she never doubted his love for her. Tom was a great provider, and Karen knew she and the kids were always his top priority.

Karen and Tom had faced many challenges over the years, but Karen was still 100 percent devoted to Tom. She always knew where she stood with him. He was never one to beat around the bush and preferred to *get right to the point.* His only fault was his *ambition.* He had a one-track mind, so if he set his mind on something, he intended to win at all costs. He would always work zealously toward his goals. If there is a negative side to his nature his criticism and judgement can raise its head.

Keywords/Phrases: No pushover, air of authority, man of his word, commands great respect, fair and just, iron fist tyrant, brilliant mind, inventive, highly intelligent, man of authority, gets right to the point, ambitious.

Further Interpretations: Great mind, CEO, diplomatic, can be harsh, strategic, and authoritarian.

Visual Representation: The King of Swords is the man and expects to be obeyed. He sits in stillness, enforcing calm and peace. He is the master of order and stability. This ruler is the epitome of intellectual power and represents judgment, command, and rulership. He achieves what he sets out to do and accomplishes all of his desires. He is a symbol of power and superiority, which may assist you on your individual life quests.

V

THE MAJOR ARCANA

THE MAJOR
ARCANA

"Every stage of life leads to the next one, and even if we try to stop the hands of time and remain in one comfortable place, it is not in our power as mortals to stop the moving cycle of life. Therefore, the end is only the beginning of something else, so the cycle of life begins once again."

On first entering the house, Tom noticed the stillness and quietness.

"Oh, that's right," he said to himself, suddenly remembering he was home alone for the first time in a while. Karen was away for the night visiting her parents, and Isac and Alice were out partying with friends. The only sound Tom could hear was the crackling of the tin roof as the temperature outside began to drop. It had been another scorching, blistering-hot day, and Tom was relieved to be home after surviving both the heat and the busyness of chasing leads and suppliers for his business. He was exhausted from the many times he had to get in and out of his car throughout the day, but he felt satisfied that it was a successful one.

Karen had thoughtfully left a dish of last night's curry in the fridge for dinner, along with reheating instructions on the refrigerator door. Tom, feeling beat, poured himself a larger than usual glass of scotch and sat at the dining table alone. He wasn't hungry at all, but he tried his best to finish as much of Karen's famous curry as possible. After forcing down as much as he could, Tom rose from the table and scraped the leftovers into the family dog's bowl. He placed his dirty dish in the dishwasher and settled down in front of the TV with a fresh glass of scotch.

"What a day," Tom said with a sigh. He kicked off his shoes in front of the air cooler, softly closed his eyes, and rested his weary head against his old, worn-out recliner. Tom loved that chair. It belonged to his pop and had definitely seen better days; the leather was faded and torn in many places. Karen often talked about tossing it out, but she knew Tom would be devastated, so there it sat, a thorn in her decor.

Settling down for a quiet night in, Tom took a long, deep breath in. It had been a while since he'd felt so at peace. Relaxing and listening to the creaking of the roof above, Tom's mind began to wander. He reminisced about his life, his family, and how strange the house felt without them. The only other time Tom recalled spending time in the house on his own was when Karen and Alice spent a week holidaying in Fiji. He was so grateful for his wonderful family, and a soft smile passed his lips as he took a small sip of his refreshing scotch. There was something about sitting in his pop's chair that always made Tom's mind reflect back to his childhood and all the wonderful, fun times he had on his grandparents' farm. He began to recall a story Nana Flo, or Gran as he called her, often told him as a small boy. She called it "21 Doors." Tom was about ten years old when he first heard the tale of the twenty-one doors.

"Behind each of the twenty-one doors lies a rich understanding of where you are in life," Gran would say. She was clearly a visionary and often knew what was happening in young Tom's life long before he did. He could clearly remember spending nights sitting by the fire at his grandparents' farm.

Nana Flo was everything to Tom; he thought the world of her. As children, he and Kenny, Tom's younger brother, spent every school holiday at her and Pops's farm. Their parents worked long hours and decided it would be safer to leave the boys at the farm than have them both roaming the streets while they were at work all day. Tom and Kenny looked forward to every holiday. They loved spending time with Gran and Pops just as much as Gran loved having them over.

Tom often thought of his Nana Flo. She was quite a big lady and loved to cook. He remembered that she always wore an apron she made from the most outrageous fabrics that defied her age. At that moment, treasured memories of watching Gran bake flashed back to him. Suddenly, he was back in her kitchen all over again. The smell of freshly baked bread filled him with comfort and love. Those kinds of memories always surfaced when he passed by the local bakery; there was something about the smell of freshly baked bread and cakes that always caused lots of fond memories to flood back in. The bonds of unconditional love never fade.

Taking another sip of his scotch, Tom recalled the nights on the farm when his Nana Flo would wrap him and his brother Kenny in warm, woollen Native blankets; light some amazing-smelling incense that wafted into their nostrils; and give them mugs of sweet hot chocolate to sip on. When they were settled, she would ask, "Where are you? What door are you about to walk through? What have you learned?"

Tom smiled as he remembered answering, "Door sixteen, Gran, the Tower."

"And what's happening?" Nana Flo asked.

"The shit has hit the fan," he said, looking up to see Nana Flo laughing.

Smiling to himself as his mind took him down memory lane, Tom began to wonder what door he was standing in front of now and what other doors he had walked through over the course of his forty-two years on Earth. He pondered all he had learned, how each experience had changed him, and how much he had grown as not only a businessman but a husband and father too. Tom could clearly see what Nana Flo had taught him all those years ago. All the parallels between the stages of his life and the lessons behind each door were quite obvious to him now.

Tom thought back to a time when he was standing at door zero, "the door of *the Fool*," as Gran called it many times over his young life.

Gran would say, "The Fool's *innocent, raw energy* is within all of us. It signifies the great beginning of *life's big adventure* and the excitement of starting off on a *new journey*. However, the Fool has *no experience*. He is naive when it comes to this new pursuit, but his energy is high, and he's *full of good intentions*. He is a *free spirit, carefree,* and *willing to take risks* while following his calling. The Fool is *up for any new challenge* and is ready to take a massive *leap of faith, fearlessly stepping into the unknown.* He's hopeful about his ability to survive anything he confronts. Is he brave or just foolish?" Gran would then add that the Fool's new journey would open up many doors, twenty-one of them to be exact, and behind every door, the Fool would confront every aspect within himself, every lesson needed to master wholeness, collective consciousness, and truth. The Fool is always ready and willing to jump headfirst into the unknown. He has no expectations, but he recognises that his path is full of possibilities and potential.

"The twenty-one doors reflect the journey of the Fool in all of us," Nana Flo would say.

Tom reflected back on one of the many times he played the part of the Fool well. One cold winter night, Karen invited her parents, Dot and Peter, to dinner so she and Tom could tell them all about their plans to start their own business. Over the years, Tom had built a good relationship with Peter and Dot and valued their opinions. They were both hardworking straight shooters, which Tom admired, and he knew he could count on them to offer sound advice. After the dishes were washed and put away and everyone was relaxing by the fire with a hot cup of coffee, Tom explained his new ideas.

Peter and Dot listened intently to what Tom had to say; they didn't interrupt him once. This alone gave Karen reason to be concerned. When Tom had finished explaining his business plan, from leasing a storefront to purchasing stock and the financials involved, Peter advised Tom to tread lightly and consider everything that could go wrong.

"You know, there is something to be said about working nine to five and getting a wage every week," Peter said.

Tom respected their old-school opinions, but his mind was made up, and he was prepared to *take the risk and follow his heart.* Tom looked only through fresh eyes at the new possibilities this venture could bring to him and his family. He was done playing it safe with his current nine-to-five. He had grown past being a slave to someone else's business. He felt empowered to follow his own path in life and was enthusiastic and excited to get the ball rolling. Others' opinions would have no impact on his decisions. Unbeknownst to him, Tom had a lot to learn and was woefully unprepared for the workload he was to encounter. Nonetheless, he refused to let his lack of experience hold him back.

Tom was an original; some may say a little eccentric. This was something Karen absolutely adored about him. He was a hard person to sway once his mind was made up, but Tom was comfortable in his skin and neither wanted nor needed others' approval. He was well known for doing his own thing; he simply did not live his life according to the needs and expectations of others.

Dot and Peter were concerned and tried to talk with Karen later that night when Tom left to go to the bathroom. Karen reassured them that Tom knew what he was doing and that they shouldn't worry. Later that evening, Karen relayed her parents' fears to Tom and told him she was proud of him for having the courage to *follow his dreams* no matter what anyone had to say.

As tired and beat as Tom felt that night, he couldn't help but reflect back on all of the twenty-one doors, what each one represented to him, and how they coexisted within his life.

I have to tell Isac and Alice the story of the twenty-one doors, Tom thought to himself. *Gran would like that.* Tom lost his beautiful gran quite a few years back, and not a day went by that he didn't recall a trinket of wisdom she passed on to him. Telling Isac and Alice the story would be a great way to keep her memory alive.

Tom rested his head and began to recall the entire story. Tom and Kenny once knew it by heart, as it was one of their favourites when they visited the farm. Every night, they would sit wrapped in their snuggly blankets as Gran told them of the adventures of the Fool.

Keywords/Phrases: Innocent raw energy, life's new big adventure, new journey, inexperienced, high energy, full of good intentions, free spirit, carefree, willing to take risks, up for a new challenge, leap of faith, stepping into the unknown, ready and willing to take a risk, follow your heart and dreams.

Further Interpretations: Fresh start, innocence, spontaneity, beginnings, no baggage, purity, optimism. Pure potential, no expectations, curiosity, individualization.

THE MAGICIAN.

"So," Gran would start, "the Fool, amidst ambiguity and excitement, opens the first of his twenty-one doors. Here, he encounters *the Magician,* door number one." Tom loved the Magician as a boy and could still picture him with his top hat and wand. Gran would describe him as a magical man who revealed to the Fool that *anything was possible.* The Magician enlightened the Fool about his *abilities to achieve something huge.*

The Magician told the Fool that, within himself, *he possessed everything he needed to turn his dreams into reality,* including passion, finances, intellect, and spirit. After meeting the Magician, the Fool was sure that his journey was possible. He felt capable of far more than he knew, and he trusted that he was *divinely guided* on his journey.

Tom could definitely recall feeling like he had met the Magician when he first put his plans of opening his store into action. He knew that if he wanted it bad enough, anything was possible.

Thinking back to his gran, Tom could hear her ask again, "Where are you? What have you learned?" Standing at door one, Tom recalled *feeling invincible.* All his *plans* had begun to *manifest, as if by magic.* The storefront he liked was available for lease, and the bank was behind him and supported his vision for the future. Tom had so much *passion and energy* for his new business, and he felt even better knowing Karen was there to back him

100 percent. Both of them were *full of inspiration* and ready to manifest the dream life they often talked about in bed at night.

Tom explained to Karen that he felt like he was called to own his own business to fulfil his *life purpose*. He could feel he was on the path toward success. For once, Tom knew that all his ducks were lined up and nothing could go wrong. He confidently moved forward with faith in his plans. Although he was excited, he knew there would be times when he would need to ask for advice, and he was *open to learning* new skills. He appreciated everyone who had contributed to helping his plans become a reality.

The magician in Tom helped him become a *good communicator,* and as a result, he mixed well with others. He neither felt above nor below his peers. He believed he possessed a natural ability to know what others thought or felt, and he prided himself on being *well-liked*. Fortunately, this side of his personality was greatly appreciated by his customers.

Keywords/Phrases: Anything is possible, capabilities, huge potential, has everything needed, turn dreams into a reality, divinely guided, feeling invincible, plans manifest by magic, passion, energy, full of inspiration, life purpose, open to learning, good communicator, well-liked.

Further Interpretations: Potential, action, initiative, higher self, wisdom, new direction, information. Partnership with spirit, communication and timing.

THE HIGH PRIESTESS

As a young boy, Tom learned to always *listen to his gut* and value the feeling within that knew exactly what he needed to do and what *felt right*. This led him to recall door two, where his understanding of the physical and spiritual worlds began to take shape.

Gran would say, "At door two, the Fool now meets *the High Priestess*. Behind this door is a *very wise woman* who is *in tune with all six of her senses*. She teaches the Fool that not everything that is real can be seen, and she shows him the importance of *trusting his intuition* and gut feelings. He must have *faith* that the universe only wants the best for him, and everything in life will appear within *divine timing* and of the *highest good*.

"She teaches the Fool to have *patience, to be still and listen*, as the answers he seeks are within. She reveals to the Fool that not everything he needs to know can be found in books or outside sources. Most of what he needs to know will come from his *intuition, his inner voice*."

This inner knowing taught Tom the art of reading between the lines to see the truth in all matters. He had always trusted the inner depths of his mind, paying particular attention to his gut feelings and inner psychic messages. Tom had the wonderful ability of *foresight*, using it to eradicate problems before they arose. Using his *wise insight*, he knew what needed to happen before the situation called for it outright, thus avoiding many disasters.

His gran had the same ability and taught him to always

remain *open-minded* and accepting of all. Gran would tell Kenny and Tom to be at peace knowing that their inner guidance would never fail them.

"Our intuition is our first sense," Gran said. "It allows us to sense the invisible, the unspoken. This is not intellect; it is where you recognize certain things and just know they are true. Your intuition is a moment of *clarity, an epiphany.*"

Gran opened Tom's eyes to the unseen and taught both him and Kenny how to meditate when they were young. It was a practice Tom had let go of, but he knew it was something he should rekindle. Thinking back to the hours he spent sitting in Gran's garden under the old birch tree brought forth other fond memories. Tom's mind flashed to the familiar smell of freshly cut grass as he saw himself sitting cross-legged among Gran's beautiful roses. Tom was amazed at how Gran got him and his brother to sit still for so long, but she had her ways; the boys always did whatever she asked, even if it was torture.

Keywords/Phrases: Listen to your gut, in tune with all six senses, trust your intuition, faith in the universe, divine timing, highest good, patience, be still and listen, intuition, inner voice, foresight, wise insight, open-minded, moment of clarity/epiphany.

Further Interpretations: Secrets, alchemy, mystery, trust yourself, meditation, psychic and spiritual development, go within to find the answers, spiritual insight, hidden wisdom, co-create.

Behind door number three was *the Empress*. Tom recalled that this was the part of the story where the Fool met the *Great Goddess*, the *Great Mother within* us all.

"She represents our connection with Mother Earth and embodies everything related to *fertility, nurturing, and abundance*. She teaches the Fool *patience and gentleness*, helping him *feel safe and secure. A marriage or birth* could be in the cards, or the situation could point to a deep emphasis on the mother."

Tom sat still, slowly sipping his scotch, lost in the memories of all the lessons he had learned from door number three, the Empress. He knew for certain that the Empress gave him all his *creativity* and the ability to *look beyond the norm*. He was never one to remain idle, and when he started his new business, he felt *capable, supported, and nurtured*.

The Empress instilled a love of nature in Tom; he loved taking long walks *outdoors*. She reminded him to take time to *stop and smell the roses* and enjoy life every now and then. She taught him to be kind to himself and connect with all the beauty and happiness within. He remembered the feelings of love and nurturing that the all-embracing arms of the Empress exuded. As a child, Tom believed Gran was the Empress in disguise, considering how much she taught him and his brother about the importance of connecting to their *sensuality* so they could attract happiness and joy into their lives.

Tom spent a few moments reflecting on his life and the lessons door three taught him. He thought of all the love he had in his own life, of Karen and the kids. With the Empress, Tom felt safe and secure, wrapped in her nurturing arms. *Good fortune* surrounded him both creatively and materially. He was passionate about putting all his ideas to work and appreciating the beautiful things hard work could bring. The Empress gave Tom the gift of determination to get things done.

Keywords/Phrases: Fertility, nurturing, abundance, patience, gentleness, safety, security, marriage, birth, creativity, look beyond the norm, capable, supported, love of nature, smell the roses, sensuality, good fortune.

Further Interpretations: Pregnancy, parenting, feminine, harmony, maternal, mother figure, fertility, natural evolution.

THE EMPEROR.

The Emperor was behind door number four. Gran would say this was when the Fool met his *father figure*.

"The Emperor teaches the Fool the *importance of order and structure*. He sets *rules and regulations* to ensure that his path is *safe and stable*. He reminds the Fool of the importance of *traditions* and remaining *grounded* as he navigates his new level of independence. The Emperor is full of *logic and reason*, a man who stands firm in his decisions. He is the *boss* and is *to be obeyed*."

Gran often called Pops the Emperor because he could be headstrong and hot-tempered at times. Pops liked things done according to his carefully laid plans and would get quite upset if things didn't go the way he hoped. It was Pops's way or the highway, and with that thought, Tom realised he had inherited this desire for results above all else.

Tom recalled that Pops was very strict, and he and Kenny would sometimes hide when he came inside for dinner. He was a big man, or so he seemed to them as kids, and he had many rules that he loved to preach to Tom and Kenny when they visited. But Tom learned a lot from Pops. If he said he was going to do something, he did it; he always followed through.

Pops was always an *authoritarian*, a man you shouldn't mess with. He taught Tom to value *structure, discipline, and responsibility*. Tom sometimes thought Pops made more of an impression on him than Gran. He was an extremely hard worker; sometimes it was well after dark before he made it inside for dinner.

One time, Pops said, "There are three types of people in this world, Tom and Kenny. The first kind is the people who make things happen. The second kind is the people who watch things happen. And the third kind is the ones who wonder what happened." Pops sure was the first kind of person.

Creativity and ideas are wonderful, but without order and logic, things can very quickly turn into chaos—that Tom knew for sure. Pops the Emperor taught him responsibility, how to be *fair and just* to gain *respect* from his peers. This made Tom think about what Isac and Alice thought of him as a father, and he hoped his *leadership and solidity* had gained their respect. Tom recalled a time when Gran talked with him and his brother about Pops. She would say that all great leaders are known for their *indomitable will, accountability*, and their ability to *get the job done.*

Keywords/Phrases: Father figure, order and structure, rules and regulations, safe and stable, grounded, traditional, logic and reason, stand firm in decisions, boss, to be obeyed, authoritarian, disciplined, fair and just, respected, responsible, leader, solidity, indomitable will, accountability, gets the job done.

Further Interpretations: Strict, takes control, ruthless, down-to-earth, strategic, masculine, follows the rules, power, reliability.

THE HIEROPHANT.

"But the twenty-one doors offer a journey, and when one door closes," Gran would say, "another door opens. It is now time for the Fool to leave his father and look for teachers who have gone before him to learn about who he really is as a person. Here, he encounters *the Hierophant* at door number five.

"The Fool is now *seeking answers* of a *philosophical kind*, an inner vision into his spirit. The Hierophant teaches the Fool to change his opinion of life to that of no opinion. He must move forward and be his own man, separate from his mother and father's protection. He advises the Fool to *pursue knowledge and seek out masters* who can help him on his journey."

In the beginning of his career as a business owner, it was difficult for Tom to relax and *conform* to the existing rules and regulations of the business world. He sure made it hard on Karen, but they eventually compromised, and he learned when it was best to step off his high horse and not rock the boat. Tom thought about all his *mentors* and appreciated everything they did to help him on his path. He was especially appreciative of his former boss, Tony, who was so valuable to Tom in the beginning of his entrepreneurial journey. He was always there to steer Tom in the right direction, and he even helped him decide what products to order for his store. At door five, Tom learned to *seek out knowledge, gain great strength and wisdom, and accept support from* people who were more knowledgeable than him.

Gran once said, "Everyone and everything around you are your *teachers*. Welcome their teachings, as they have the keys to unlock the doors *to a higher understanding.*"

The Hierophant, as Tom recalled, is the *wisdom giver who offers advice* about which way to go without forcing their opinion. Tony was Tom's hierophant, *wise beyond his years* and always ready to *offer advice* when needed.

Keywords/Phrases: Seeking philosophical answers, pursue knowledge, seek out masters, conform, mentors, great strength, wisdom, support, higher understanding, wisdom giver, offers advice, wise beyond years.

Further Interpretations: Go deep within, stimulate inner healing, education, study, tradition, conventional, good advice, spiritual leadership.

"Craving companionship on his travels, the Fool begins looking for *a partner*. It can be a lonely world out there if you let it be," Gran would say. "So, the Fool discovers the first major *choice* of his life at door number six. Here, he meets *the Lovers*. The consequences of choices in life are enormous. The Fool must *think clearly and act wisely,* as the implications of his choices could cause much heartache."

The Lovers reminded Tom that it was wise to always *follow his heart*, for "love is magical and a miracle," Gran would say. Tom thought back to what his life was like before he met Karen. He remembered he had big plans to travel the world. He would lie awake night after night planning his big trip. His friends often said he was spontaneous, and they envied his sense of adventure. He was also a bit of a ladies' man—or so he thought. He was so far away from settling down, but his life took a detour when he met Karen. Tom knew he had met his *soulmate and life partner.* He felt blessed in ways that were hard to express, and he knew, without a doubt, that he was meant to make *a connection* with her that would change him in ways he could not possibly imagine. He could trust her completely and knew their *partnership* would move mountains. Tom knew that committing to Karen would have a huge impact on his future travel plans, but not a day went by that he had any regrets.

Tom chose to stay and, as a result, sacrificed his travelling desires. He remembered his gran telling him to never be afraid to step into the role his heart was leading him to. So, he committed and never looked back. Tom thought about the *strong bond* he and Karen shared and how they *gave each other strength and confidence.* His choice to stay and court Karen was divinely guided by Gran, and marrying her was life-changing in the most positive way.

Keywords/Phrases: Partnership, choice, think clearly, act wisely, follow your heart, soulmate, life partner, a connection, strong bond, give each other strength and confidence.

Further Interpretations: Deep love, the strength of two people, commitment, oneness.

Tom sat for a while and thought of all the fond memories he and Karen made throughout their twenty-year relationship. Their journey through life together reminded him that, up to this point, the Fool had learned so much on his journey too. He was now at door number seven, where he would meet *the Chariot.*

Gran's story continued: "The Fool begins to *pull all his resources together,* using *willpower and discipline* to remain *focused and on track*. He is now *planning and moving five*, six steps ahead. Life is *all systems go* and *keeps moving forward*. It's time for the Fool to take hold of the reins, so to speak. His goals are within his sights, and he has developed a *great determination* to keep going. *The Chariot* is a sign that he can *achieve anything* he wants with enough *ambition and drive.*"

With Karen by his side, Tom felt that anything was possible. His biggest motivator in life was to always be the first type of man in Pops's story, never the third. The Chariot reminded Tom of all the hard work, determination, *commitment,* and drive he and Karen had put into their marriage and business over the years. They had come up against many *challenges and detours* but always *kept their goal in sight,* pushing through, staying focused, and maintaining control with *self-discipline* and their high *drive to succeed.*

Tom smiled. He was most definitely aboard the Chariot when he decided to follow his ambitions and start his own business. He recalled the many challenges and obstacles he overcame in the early days by keeping his focus and maintaining his *willpower* and determination. There was so much to do during those years, and at times, it felt like he was herding cats. But he and Karen continued to put their heads together and move on with the task at hand, even in times of adversity. Tom felt like he *rode victoriously through life* at that stage. He was determined to show Karen's parents that all their worries and concerns were unnecessary.

Keywords/Phrases: Pulls all his resources together, willpower, discipline, focused, on track,
planning and moving, all systems go, moving
forward, great determination, can achieve anything, ambition, drive, commitment, challenges,
detours, keep goals in sight, maintain control,
self-discipline, drive to succeed, ride victoriously
through life.

Further Interpretations: Direction, inner turbulence, struggles within, being pulled apart, victory, a journey, action, progress, balance, courage, inherent success.

Tom took another sip of his scotch
and remembered that the Fool was
now moving on to door number
eight, where he would meet
Strength. Whenever Tom or
Kenny were on the verge of having
hissy fits as children—usually over
something trivial—Gran would
say, "Open door eight. On the
Fool's journey, he developed the
courage to tame the childlike tan-
trums going on within. Strength
showed the Fool how to handle his rage and *master self-discipline*,
to *put pride and ego aside* for his highest good. Through this

inner strength, he understood that some battles were not worth the effort. He *matured* and started to value *self-control.* With Strength, he was able to see his *boundaries and limitations* and had amazing restraint and *patience."*

When Tom thought about Strength, he thought about the *big steps* he had taken throughout life and the *bold* career moves he confidently undertook. Leaving his safe nine-to-five to branch out on his own showed massive inner strength. He had grown considerably and had become more compassionate, kind, caring, and patient over the years. Where once Tom was quick to overreact, he was now able to channel his energies, passion, and anger to work *for* him, not against him.

Tom knew he was not the easiest man to live with. There were many times Karen had to call on her inner strength to tame the beast of Tom's ambitions. Karen's *resilience and fearlessness* often put Tom in his place. She never had an issue with speaking her mind and letting him know exactly what she thought of his behaviour, especially when he was becoming impossible to deal with and was making himself sick.

His relationship with Karen grew stronger year after year and was filled with *empathy, pride, and mutual confidence.* Tom was a strong match for Karen, but at times, he had to dig deep to find the strength to make sense of his self-sabotaging ways. Tom recalled the hard times and gave thanks for the *endurance* he mustered from behind the shadows to *go the distance.*

Keywords/Phrases: Inner strength, courage, master self-discipline, put pride and ego aside, mature, self-control, boundaries, limitations, patience, big steps, bold, compassionate, kind, caring, resilience, fearless, empathy, pride, confidence, endurance, go the distance.

Further Interpretations: Taming the beast within, self-love, unconditional love, self-respect, know your capabilities.

At the next door, number nine, the Fool encountered *the Hermit,* "The *wise old man,*" Gran called him. "The Fool now *seeks solitude* in order to go within and reflect on everything he has learned so far. He *retreats* to be in *isolation, find silence, and seek guidance.* The Fool now begins to realize that *everything is connected and divinely planned* by the universe. There is a plan, a path, and a time for everything.

"*The Hermit* has taught the Fool the benefits of *meditation and stillness,* of *detaching* from your small self and *listening for guidance.* This is a time for remembering where you have been, the lessons you have learned, and who you truly are. It's a time of no outer chaos," Gran would say. "Within this quiet time, the Fool has developed a firm *sense of identity* and a deep respect for his limitations. He understands that the passing of time is a natural cycle; he cannot force the tides. *Silence isn't empty; it is full of answers.*"

Tom recognized that he was currently at door number nine as he sat in solitude, enjoying his scotch and appreciating his *time alone* and away from the demands of his life. Tom had always thought of himself as a quiet, modest, and private person who valued time alone to work through his thoughts and *clear his mind.* That night, sitting on his own, Tom had been given a sense of *heightened insight.* He began to draw his attention inward to look for all the answers he sought. He recognized how deeply he had committed to his business, and he finally had time to *declutter* his mind, regroup and align once again with his true self, his true purpose. He searched his inner soul for guidance on where he should go next, and this time alone was something he only just realized he was in great need of.

Tom came to the realization that what was really important to him was his family. In facing the truth of his neglect, he had the urge to call Karen. But when he looked at his watch and saw it was close to midnight, he decided against it. Money and success were no longer what Tom needed to feel whole or be the man he wished to be.

Keywords/Phrases: Wise old man, seek solitude, go within, reflect, retreat, isolation, find silence, seek guidance, everything is connected, divinely planned, meditation, stillness, detaching, listen for guidance, sense of identity, silence isn't empty; it is full of answers, time alone, clear mind, heightened insight, declutter, align, regroup.

Further Interpretations: Find clarity within, quest for personal truth, spiritual illumination, holds the lamp to guide you, inner guidance, withdraw from pressure, wisdom, warnings, Time out, reflection, introspection, clarity, self-care, what have I learnt.

"Now that the Fool has taken some quiet time away to think," Gran continued, "he can move on to door number ten, where he will meet the *Wheel of Fortune.* Here, he must accept that everything happens due to the turning of the Wheel and that we're all subject *to fate, chance, synchronicity, and destiny.* This is the turning point of the Fool's journey, and the Wheel can *turn in any direction at any time.* This can be *good or challenging,* but whichever way the

Wheel turns will bring *growth* and a new chapter of the Fool's life."

Tom had so much to consider when standing before door ten. He pondered all the ups and downs of his life. At present, life was moving really fast. His business was taking off and the children were growing older right before his eyes and venturing into the world on their own. Karen dreaded this time in her life, but Tom trusted the universe and put his faith in the blessings of his *highest good coming* to him in due time. Tom had learned over the years that there were some things he would never have control over, and he decided to stop trying to understand everything in this lifetime. But still, he was wise enough to know that every moment of life comes with a lesson. Gran often said, "Change is not optional, but suffering is."

Where Karen was more grounded and practical, Tom welcomed change and was always on the lookout for more knowledge. Tom believed in *fate* and often told Karen they were fated to meet that day at the football field. Gran always said, "Each of us is on our own path and journey, and we cannot control that of another," but Tom believed he had grown into a better person with Karen by his side.

Tom and Karen both surrounded themselves with positive people who always showed up to help and support them when needed. Sometimes Tom felt like he had to show some sense of humility before accepting help, but regardless, he was happy and content with his lot in life. He was wise enough to not become too comfortable, as the Wheel of Fortune was *always revolving,* and he knew his *drive and passion* would surely keep life *in motion.*

Keywords/Phrases: Fate, chance, destiny, synchronicity, turning point, any direction; any time, good or challenging, growth, highest good, calming, always revolving, drive, passion, in motion.

Further Interpretations: Good fortune, luck, change in direction, unexpected cycles, karmic association, change, improvement.

It was getting late, but Tom was not ready to retire to bed just yet. He thought more about the Fool, beginning to internalize just how much life moves in a continuous cycle.

"Standing before door number eleven, the Fool meets *Justice*. Justice brings *balance* into situations and *resolution* to legal matters," Gran says. "She teaches the Fool to act with integrity because his *actions* will always *have consequences*. He must *remain impartial* in making decisions, and he must always keep his *thoughts balanced*. He must also *remain fair and just* and treat others as he would like to be treated."

Tom thought of Justice as *a balancing act*, and to be accountable for the parts he has played in life. All that had gone before him in his past and the things he experienced now reflected to his future. All the seeds he had sown and all the hard work he had endured was worth it, for he could now reap the rewards. It was not a time to run from his responsibilities; rather, it was time to stand up and take control of them. There was no need to worry, as every decision was always made, whether the outcome was favourable or not. When life's demands laid heavy on Tom's shoulders, he thought of Justice and tried his best to not play the victim.

When Tom's business took a hit from the competitor, Justice was by his side. At no time did he allow himself to be pulled down. He may have been upset for a bit, but he quickly set his emotions aside and got on with it. But Tom wasn't too proud to admit when he made a mistake and take responsibility for his actions. He was a cup-half-full kind of man. He knew there were always going to be times in life when he felt he was *being judged*. He could happily say he had *acted fairly* toward others most of the time, but he recognized moments when he could have handled some situations better.

One time, Tom lost the plot a little, causing him and Karen to butt heads. He acted incredibly defensive and kept Karen in the dark regarding his true feelings, which was something he had never done before. The tension in the house was enormous. For a while, they lost faith and trust in each other. Thankfully, they found a way to *compromise*, and the faith and respect they had toward each other returned. During that time, Tom learned that, in every relationship, there's *a time for speaking and a time for listening.* Life had a way of *balancing* his happy experiences with challenging ones. Gran would always say, "For every cause, there is an effect; you reap what you sow."

Keywords/Phrases: Balance, resolution, actions, consequences, remain impartial, balanced thoughts, fair and just, balancing act, being judged, act fairly, compromise, a time for speaking and a time for listening.

Further Interpretations: Cause and effect, the truth comes out, harmony, karma, clarity, legal situations, honesty is the best policy, accountability, karma

THE HANGED MAN.

Tom had faced door twelve, *the Hanged Man,* a few times in his life. He thought of the many times he felt the need to *surrender and pause* and *create a space* where he felt safe enough to explore the world from a *different point of view.*

"This is a time to surrender to what is and *reflect* on the now," Gran said. "This is a time for the Fool to learn to *hang back, let go of all attachments,* and be in a *moment of suspension.* He must *sacrifice* what he wants to do for his greatest good and *buy himself some time.* Life cannot always be go, go, go. The Fool must now trust that the universe will always be there to catch him. Life doesn't always have to move quickly to go well; sometimes a *pause* is more beneficial. So, *be quiet, rest and be still* for just a little while.

"At times, when things are not going as you'd like, the best thing you can do is *change the way you look at things,* then the things you look at will change. Look at everything with different eyes, and you will get a different *perspective* of where you are going and what you want," Gran would say.

The wisdom passed on from the Hanged Man had been so valuable to Tom over the years, as he had a tendency of being a bull in a china shop at times. On the flip side, Karen always knew when it was time to *take a break.* Every six months or so, she'd say enough was enough and book a weekend away at a secluded cabin while her parents watch the kids. And she was always right. Sometimes Tom tried to make an excuse as to why he couldn't take time off, but Karen never asked; it was an order.

She would say, "That is exactly why we are going. You need to *step away* for a while to *see the bigger picture.* You need to put some distance between yourself and what you are trying to achieve. If things are not turning out as you had planned or hoped, a few days away will do you good to clear your head and allow time for miracles to unfold. Come Monday morning, everything will become clearer."

She was right, but sometimes Tom couldn't see the forest for the trees no matter how much *time for reflection* he had. He recalled Gran saying, "Where there is a will, there is a way if you *step away from the outcome.*"

Tom reflected for a moment on Gran's story of the twenty-one doors and how wise she was. He wished he had appreciated her wisdom more when he was younger.

Keywords/Phrases: Surrender, pause, create space, different point of view, reflect, hang back, moment of suspension, sacrifice, buy some time, be still and quiet, change the way you look at things, perspective, take a break, see the bigger picture, step away from the outcome.

Further Interpretations: Wait, make a sacrifice for the greater good, voluntary sacrifice, wisdom, initiation, pause in one's life, obtain wisdom, free yourself from patterns.

All these thoughts of *endings* led Tom to think of door number thirteen. "Here," Gran says, "the Fool meets *Death*, and the person the Fool once thought he was is now beginning to fall away as he enters a whole new phase of his existence, a *total transformation*. He has now made room for *new opportunities* to enter his life. He has learned to let go of what was not serving him and *eliminate old habits* or associations and welcome in a *fresh start*. The Fool has learned that change is inevitable and *decay is inherent* in all things. Everything must *come to an end* to make way for a *new beginning. From death*

comes rebirth. The dark twists and turns of life will always lead you to the *light. Endings* come in many forms, so stop holding onto what must die. Trust that you are about to be reborn."

As children, Tom and Kenny were petrified of door thirteen, often having nightmares from the thought of it. That was until Gran assured them that it was a good door. She would tell the boys that Death was like cleaning out their toy box and giving away some of their old toys to *make room* for all the new ones.

"Out with the old and in with the new," Gran would say. "We must all keep advancing because if we get stuck for too long, the Death door will sneak up on us."

Over the course of his life, Tom had stood before the door of Death many times, with one of the most significant being when he and Karen decided to sell their store. They had *outgrown* that stage of their lives and were both *ready for new adventures* that allowed them to evolve. As scary as the unknown was at the time, they *embraced the change* and welcomed a new beginning. *When one door closes, another opens.*

Keywords/Phrases: Endings; total transformation; new opportunities; eliminate old habits; fresh start; change the inevitable; decay is inherent; come to an end; new beginnings; from death comes rebirth; dark and light; must die to be reborn; make room; out with the old, in with the new; adventure; embrace change; when one door closes, another opens.

Further Interpretations: Rebirth, let go and let God, transition, big changes, time to move on.

"Door fourteen, *Temperance*," Gran said. "This is where the Fool learns to *be patient and find balance* in all things. After experiencing the different challenges of life, he learns to blend, harmonise, and be at peace spiritually. The Fool can now bridge the gap to accomplish all his plans. He begins to relax and find the *flow of life* once again. It's a time to *enter calm waters*. He is now able to see both sides clearly and *compromise* to find balance and *peace*."

Temperance reminded Tom of all the life experiences that helped him understand and accept who he was and become a better man. Getting married, starting a family, and establishing his own business—all of these major decisions were what made the biggest differences in his life. He could clearly see what he wanted to do, be, and have. At Temperance's door, he felt *healed*.

"Door fourteen offers you a chance to *help yourself*, to do something and not wait for others to do it for you. You start by helping yourself and taking the first baby step," Gran said.

Temperance also reminded Tom of Karen and the *gentle*

ways she operated her life. She had mastered the art of remaining calm during stressful times, like when the business was suffering. She said she had found peace within, which allowed her to stay *patient, steady, and devoted* to her cause. She always reminded Tom that good things took time.

When Tom was under enormous stress while working at the store, he thought the world was crashing in on him. His heart would race, and he would talk himself into all sorts of chaos. Karen was the only one who could see the pressure Tom put on himself, and she worked hard to be the soft, gentle voice he needed.

Tom recalled Karen saying to him one night, "Peace is found within, and the way to peace is to accept that things are exactly how they should be. *Trust that everything will work out* and focus only on the good in your life. *Find harmony within,* and peace will find you." She always had a way with words.

Keywords/Phrases: Patience, balance, blend, harmonise, peace, spirituality, find the flow, enter calm waters, compromise, healed, help yourself, gentle ways, remaining calm, steady, devoted, trust everything will work out, find harmony within.

Further Interpretations: Cooperation, optimism, self-control, moderation, spiritual growth, love-flow balance.

Smiling, Tom thought of the next door, number fifteen, where the Fool is confronted by *the Devil*. This is another door that freaked the boys out as kids, but Gran always said, "The Fool is now forced to witness all the *self-inflicted limitations* he has placed upon himself. All his *negative thinking, guilt, shame, and bad habits* lay bare. At this door, he begins to tackle his inner demons and realises he is not completely happy with himself. He recognises aspects of himself that he has been unable to break free from and accepts that he has been living in a place of *denial*. The Fool must enter *a time of darkness* for *self-assessment* or he may remain forever *in bondage to his own fear.*

"If the Devil worries you, take your awareness back to Temperance. That will give you the courage to move on," Gran would say. "It is perfectly natural to feel this way because the Devil is a *prime manipulator*. I know exactly when I am standing before door fifteen. *My mind betrays me* and is full *of self-sabotaging thoughts, limiting beliefs, negativity, and annoyance,* which vex my soul and interrupt my sense of peace and harmony.

"Sometimes I will even invent an excuse for why I don't want to do something that I feel may push me *out of my comfort zone.* Tom recalls Gran saying, "If you feel that way, that's the devil in you. It *is holding you back, keeping you small,* and helping you *make excuses.*"

When Tom stood in front of door fifteen, he was his *own worst enemy.* He was the one who held himself back. There were many times in his life when he felt he had lost his way. When the new competitor opened up their store, Tom struggled with it, and his self-worth suffered. He felt he wasn't good enough and that he lacked the abilities to run a successful business. Faith in his store and himself eluded him. His thoughts were dark, and at times, he *lost sight of the big picture.* He felt a sense of helplessness and a deep-seated fear that he had dug himself into a hole and was trapped.

Karen was once again his saviour. She made Tom realise that all his pain was happening at his *own hands.* His *negative thinking* was only helping him stay bound, stuck, and unhappy. "All this worry is unnecessary and could be avoided if you stood up and *reclaimed your self-worth,"* she said to him one time while working in the store office. Over time, he began to see the error in his ways and *broke free* of the shackles of his *self-sabotaging mind* so he could continue moving forward toward fulfilling his dreams.

Keywords/Phrases: Self-inflicted limitations, negative thinking, guilt and shame, bad habits, inner demons, denial, time of darkness, self-assessment, bound to fear, prime manipulator, self-sabotaging, limiting beliefs, negativity and annoyance, out of comfort zone, holding you back, keeping you small, making excuses, own worst enemy, lost sight of big picture.

> **Further Interpretations:** Addictions, ego, stuck, want-to-but-can't attitude, addictive behaviours, greed, obsession, materialism, a need for control, temptations, detachment, having healthy boundaries.

THE TOWER.

"If you don't listen, you will find yourself at door number sixteen, and there, you will meet *the Tower*. The Fool is warned not to place all his faith on *shaky foundations, as life can change without any given notice by external forces* that are *totally out of your control*. This may seem terrifying, but it's in the Fool's best interest! The Tower forces the Fool to make both *inner and outer changes* and create some stability for himself. This *forced, assertive change* is a favour from the universe to help set him free. The Fool will come to realize that *unpredictable and chaotic change* is sometimes necessary; it helps build character, strength, and resilience," Gran would say.

"*Don't get too comfortable.* Just when you think you've dotted all your I's and crossed all your T's, something or someone could *unexpectedly let you down*. Door sixteen has a way of ripping the rug right out from under your feet. No matter how careful you are, you cannot stop the Tower from crumbling."

Tom was a man who liked to get things done. He often worried that if he procrastinated for too long, he would miss the opportunities presented to him. He suffered badly from FOMO, fear of missing out. If at times he ever did procrastinate, he was sure he'd welcome in a *huge wake-up call*.

Tom recalled telling Karen from his hospital bed that he was fine and that she shouldn't worry. This was the Tower's way of making me see sense. He explained to her that he had lost his way and had gotten too comfortable with the way life was with the store. The thought of selling it was scary, so the Tower brought about a mild heart attack so he could take the time to *re-evaluate his actions* and make a move. In the hospital, Tom realized he could no longer continue working the way he had been; the universe would see to it.

Gran would say, "You cannot linger in no-man's-land for too long or make assumptions on what you can expect ahead. Win or lose, there is always a lesson to be learned. *Expect the unexpected*. There are things in life that you will never have control over. Your life is preordained for a greater purpose. You cannot stop the hands of time or sit too comfortably upon your throne before your future path becomes evident." She was such a wise old lady.

Keywords/Phrases: Shaky foundation, unexpected, pull the rug right out from under you, external forces, totally out of your control, forced changes, unpredictable, chaotic change, don't get too comfortable, let down, huge wakeup call, re-evaluate actions, expect the unexpected.

Further Interpretations: Ruin, upheaval, unwanted change, sudden change, disruption, surprise, end of illusion.

THE STAR.

"After the shakedown with the Tower, the Fool opens door number seventeen to meet *the Star*. He is feeling quite *vulnerable* at this stage of his journey, having all that he had put his heart, soul, and faith into torn from him. He has lost his way after the shakedown and is unsure of his future. But within the Star *shines a light,* and he now begins to see the *light at the end of the tunnel*. This provides the Fool with *hope* and a *sense of renewal*. The Star offers the Fool some time to *heal* and *rejuvenate*. He can begin to *pick up the pieces,* dust himself off, and enter the pathway of life once again with *hope, faith,* and *courage*. The Star will always *light the way*."

When Tom's business was on the brink of collapse, he often thought of door seventeen so he could *remain hopeful* that everything would work out. Whenever Tom felt life closing in, Karen would say that everything was going to be alright, to have a little faith. She was his rock, his star, and he missed her like crazy whenever she was away. Through thick and thin, Tom could always rely on Karen. She had a way of making his *life a whole lot brighter.*

Tom glanced out the window as he sipped his scotch. He could see the stars in the night sky, and he wondered which one was Gran. Her memory was cemented in Tom's core, forever anchored in his heart. Tom hoped she was proud of him. Looking up at the stars, Tom's *worries faded* into the past and he found a *renewed purpose* within his life path.

Tom felt like he was in exactly the right place and that the stars were aligned in his favour. In Tom's eyes, *nothing could go wrong.* Karen and the kids were all happy, and this alone filled his heart. There were sure to be *good times ahead,* and Tom was prepared for whatever life had in store for him next. He was forever grateful for the choices he made in his past because they made him a very happy man.

Keywords/Phrases: Vulnerable, light at the end of the tunnel, hope, sense of renewal, heal, rejuvenate, pick up the pieces, faith, courage, light the way, remain hopeful, life is a whole lot brighter, worries fade, renewed purpose, nothing can go wrong, good times ahead.

Further Interpretations: Bright future, pick yourself up, keep the faith, truth revealed, inner clarity, miracles happen, innovation, inspiration, self-esteem, inspired action.

THE MOON.

Gran would be so happy that Tom had seen the light, but the Fool must not stop on his journey. Next was door number eighteen, where he meets *the Moon*.

"The Fool is now faced with what *fears* remain trapped or *hidden* within his subconscious," Gran would say. *"Light casts a shadow,* and the shadow, in this case, is the *old anxieties* and fears that may rise to the surface when the Fool attempts to shine brightly. He needs to have a look at what is going on within his psyche and enter parts of himself that he has been *hiding*. He may begin to have *strong dreams* that show the way and keep him from walking around in the dark. The Moon will teach him to use his *intuition* to see clearly despite others' *deceptions* and weave his way *past delusions*.

The Moon taught Tom how to *tame his fantasies* and keep his feet on the ground instead of being *fooled by his imagination*, emotions, dreams, and *illusions* on his path to fulfilment. Karen was well aware that Tom sometimes let his imagination run away with him. She often told him to "get off the moon and come back to Earth" whenever he got a bit carried away with his fantasies.

With the Moon, there is always *a shadow,* which reminded Tom that it was wise to always look at both sides of the coin; *not everything is as it seems.* Tom had enormous faith in his intuition and trusted his *instincts* whenever something did not feel right. He had a natural ability to see beyond the façade and spot deception a mile away. Over the years, Tom recalled coming face-to-face with many scams and wannabe con artists as a business owner, but not much got past his radar.

Tom knew he was a shrewd businessman, but at times he hid behind Karen's confidence and optimism. He lacked faith in himself and often faced times of *uncertainty and confusion.* Karen encouraged Tom to *face his fears* and turn his negative thoughts into something more constructive. When Tom suffered from his *demons,* he sent the store into disarray. He recalled a time he lost his way, and the atmosphere at the store became tense. Everyone was confused about their role, and Karen had to step in and remind him to take back control and not lose faith in what he started. His *old beliefs clouded his judgment.* Karen was right as usual, so Tom took back the reins, and life at the store began to run smoothly again.

> **Keywords/Phrases:** Hidden, fears, a shadow, old anxieties, hiding in the dark, strong dreams, intuition, deceptions, past delusions, fooled by imagination, tame fantasies, illusions, not everything is

as it seems, instincts, uncertainty, confusion, face your fears, internal demons, old habits, clouding your judgment.

Further Interpretations: Escapism, subconscious, unknown, not sure what is going on, pay attention to your dreams, self-deceit, unseen problems, trust your intuition.

THE SUN .

"All is good when the Fool arrives at door number nineteen and meets *the Sun,*" Gran would say. "The Fool is now feeling a full sense of *renewal* and complete *rejuvenation.* He has *seen the light* and has come out into the open to shine, and *shine* he does. He *illuminates the path forward* for others and himself with a feeling of *consciousness rising.* This is a time of *great joy and happiness,* for the Fool is almost at the end of his journey. He has mastered all the lessons of life, whether joyful or tough, and it's *time to celebrate.* The Fool rejoices that *life is good.*"

Scotch in hand, Tom reflected on his life and realized that it has been a wonderful ride, and it couldn't get any better. He could not be happier with how his life had turned out. He felt like *anything was possible* and nothing could stand in his way. He had the same feelings not long after opening the store; he felt *invincible.*

That night, sitting with his scotch, he felt *joy* for every aspect of his life. Tom could honestly say he was *content* and able to embrace the feeling of liberation that came with being *happy* for the sake of pure happiness. Tom was aware that these feelings were not from outside of himself but purely from within.

Sipping his scotch, Tom's mind travelled back to his childhood and the times he spent with Gran and Pops on their farm. He loved to wake up early before the roosters started crowing. Gran was usually already up, busy baking in the kitchen to beat the heat. Tom remembered Gran pouring him a glass of cold milk as he sat on the kitchen stool to watch her fuss about in the kitchen.

Tom recalled the day he married Karen. He knew his heart was where it was meant to be and that the grass was greenest exactly where he was standing. *Nothing felt better* than saying "I do" to her. Their love was so powerful, Tom knew he would never be the same man again. They were in *true alignment* with each other; they had been and always would be. Tom knew half of himself was missing that night with Karen away from home, but he was not sad. He was happy in his own skin, and having his wife in his life was the icing on the cake.

Tom loved door nineteen the most out of all twenty-one doors. Nothing could go wrong; *life was great.* Tom had grown so much and knew exactly where his strengths lied; he felt invincible. All his plans, hopes, and dreams had fallen into place. Tom knew he was knocking on door nineteen when he opened his store. It felt like everything he touched turned to gold. There were a few hurdles, but they were nothing he couldn't overcome. At this point of the story, young Tom always wanted Gran to stop so they could revel in the good feelings the Sun brought, but Gran would say, "Not yet; the Fool still has two lessons to go."

Keywords/Phrases: Renewal, rejuvenation, see the light, shine, illuminate path forward, consequences, great joy, happiness, time to celebrate, life is good, anything is possible, invincible, content, happy, nothing feels better, true alignment, life is great.

Further Interpretations: Good fortune, material happiness, success, good outcome, positive, vitality, growth, full of inspiration.

JUDGEMENT.

"So, the Fool moves on and approaches door number twenty to meet *Judgment*. The Fool can see a *universal transformation* happening, not just with the world around him but *within* himself as well. He notices a *big change* within and realises he has *grown spiritually* and has been awakened to his *life purpose*. This is a huge *developmental milestone*, and he feels the need to *rise up* and answer his *true calling*.

This is *Judgment Day,* where he is now held accountable for everything he has created and done in his past. The Fool is *awakening* to fulfil his spiritual quest, equipped with life experiences. He has a *clear perception* of all that he is and all that he will be."

Tom looked forward to Karen's return. He missed her when she was away and hated the amount of time he had to spend on the road when they owned the store. He knew it was essential for their growth, but it didn't feel right to be apart from Karen for so long. Tom was aware that every day of his life had led him to this wonderful moment. *Unlimited opportunities* were available for the couple. They had sold their store, paid off all their debts, and the kids were grown and busy with their own lives. The time was ripe for them to relax, enjoy the moment, and *wait for the will of the universe* to lead them on their next great journey.

Tom felt like he had learned all the great lessons Nana Flo had taught him all those years ago. He had stood the test of time, his *energy was renewed*, and his heart was full of *enthusiasm*. What could possibly go wrong? Tom sat and pondered all the mistakes he had made in his life and found space for forgiveness. He evaluated his past actions and found peace with a *clearer understanding* of what he needed to change about himself. Those changes would lead him to find his *true self.*

As usual, Gran was right. All the highs and lows of life, or the Fool's great journey, were about to end, and Tom knew he was currently standing in front of door twenty. Life was about to offer up the *unimaginable*. Anything was possible. Tom could feel a big change in the wind and welcomed it with open arms. *Miracles beckoned*, and *new opportunities* were abundant. All was well, and Tom had all the energy he needed to feel *renewed.* He had every reason to feel optimistic. He had passed the test of time and liked where he was headed.

Keywords/Phrases: Universal transformation within, big change, grown spiritually, life purpose, developmental milestones, rising up, true calling, Judgment Day, awakening, clear perception, unlimited opportunities, wait for the will of the universe, energy renewed, enthusiasm, clear understanding, true self, unimaginable miracles, new opportunities.

Further Interpretations: Wakeup call, clarity, positive action, rebirth, final decision, transformation, new life, a calling, accountability, purpose.

"Finally, the Fool reaches the last of his doors, door number twenty-one, *the World.* This is the end of the Fool's journey," Gran would say. "The Fool feels a sense of *achievement and triumph,* of *wholeness, completeness, and acceptance.* The Fool has *reached his goal* and has made it to the *end of the great cycle* of life. But whenever we arrive at the end, a fresh challenge arises. After this, the Fool will set out once again to begin where he started. The World is *complete*, but *the end is the catalyst for a new beginning.*"

Tom enjoyed the moment, reflecting for a while on how far he'd come. Never before had he taken so much time to ponder exactly what wisdom and lessons the twenty-one doors offered him. He felt as if he was standing on top of a great mountain with a birds-eye view of his past. Tom ran his eye over his motives and opportunities and the people who entered his life to be a part of his great journey. That night, a great wave of *awareness* and *gratitude* swept over him, and he silently shed a tear.

"Thank you, Gran," Tom whispered. He said a little prayer, thanking his angels for their guidance and interventions, for getting him where he was in his life. He knew he could not have done it without their support and love. He had *come full circle,* and he knew his gran would be proud of him.

Gran once said, "You will know when you reach home because you can radically accept yourself and everything your journey has presented to you to date, including all the successes and failures."

As a small boy, Tom always wondered what his gran was trying to say, but that night, he could see the divinity in her words. There was *no beginning without an ending.* So, just when Tom thought he was *content* and settled, giving himself credit for a *job well done,* he was faced with door twenty-one, the World, and had no choice but to wonder what the future had in store for him next.

"Bring it on," he said aloud.

Keywords/Phrases: Achievement, triumphs, wholeness, completeness, acceptance, reached goals, end of a cycle, the end is a catalyst for a new beginning, awareness and gratitude, come full circle, no beginning without an ending, well done, contentment.

Further Interpretations: Victory, fulfilment, completion, you made it, successful, happy ending, travel, self-mastery.

Afterword

I hope by now you are beginning to connect with each of the seventy-eight cards on a much deeper level. My wish is that you continue to journal the meanings, keywords, and phrases that come to mind as your Tarot experience grows. Your interpretations may change as your intuition develops over time.

The biggest piece of advice I would like to extend to you is to trust your voice. My meanings, keywords, and phrases may differ from your interpretations or what you have read in other Tarot books. That is perfectly OK. Connecting with your own interpretations is the most important aspect of memorising the cards' essences. If a card holds a certain meaning for you, trust that. Remember, you are the one reading the cards. A meaning will always be easier to remember when it is made within your subconscious mind rather than simply read in an external source. Don't get bogged down trying to memorise other people's meanings. They will never stick. Simply use them as a guide to make your own connections. Create a story for yourself or link a card to a life event so your subconscious mind has something to connect with. Also, be sure to keep the core elements of each suit and the cards' numerology in mind if that helps.

Mastering card reading will allow you to always have insight into the cycles of your life and the lives of others. It can reveal the many trials and tribulations you may face on your path and can help you make big decisions along the way. Just relax, and remember there are no right or wrong meanings, only the meanings you give them. So, as Gran would say, "Go for it, have fun, and enjoy the journey!"

About the Author

Certified hypnotherapist and past life regressionist, Jo Galloway has been a student of the Tarot for over thirty-five years. She lives on the beautiful Mid North Coast of NSW Australia with her husband and their many farm animals. Jo is a lover of the outdoors, having spent thirty years of her life working with horses. She is also the creator of the blog *Pillars of Divinity*, where she expresses her passion for mysticism and spirituality, and she's on a mission to create the esoteric for everyday.

Download Your Free Ebook

Scan the QR code with your phone!

Thank you for reading 21 Doors, A Tarot Story.
If you enjoyed this book, please help spread
the word by leaving an online review.

KEEP IN TOUCH WITH JO GALLOWAY

Website: www.pillarsofdivinity.com
Facebook: @pillarsofdivinity
Instagram: @pillarsofdivinity

Printed in Great Britain
by Amazon

42743505R00145